LISTS TO LIVE BY

~⌒⌐

"*Lists to Live By* books condense *big* truths into one-page packages. Read one list a day and you'll be wiser for it."

BRUCE WILKINSON, BESTSELLING AUTHOR, *THE PRAYER OF JABEZ*

"By recapturing the essence of good common sense, this book gives me a pain-free self-improvement plan. *Lists to Live By* span time, fortune, and fame and affirm that more things are going *well* than it sometimes seems."

SUSAN S. EAMES, PRESIDENT, THE CEDARWOOD GROUP

"Another excellent, helpful book of lists, filled with practical advice based on biblical principles."

KENNETH TAYLOR, CHAIRMAN, TYNDALE HOUSE PUBLISHERS

LISTS TO LIVE BY: THE FOURTH COLLECTION
published by Multnomah Publishers, Inc.

Cover design by The DesignWorks Group

Unless otherwise indicated, Scripture quotations are from:
The Holy Bible, New International Version © 1973, 1984 by International Bible Society,
used by permission of Zondervan Publishing House

Other Scripture quotations are from:
Holy Bible, New Living Translation (NLT) © 1996. Used by permission of Tyndale House
Publishers, Inc. All rights reserved.

The Holy Bible, New King James version (NKJV) © 1984 by Thomas Nelson, Inc.

Multnomah is a trademark of Multnomah Publishers, Inc.,
and is registered in the U.S. Patent and Trademark Office.
The colophon is a trademark of Multnomah Publishers, Inc.

Lists To Live By is a trademark of Multnomah Publishers
and is registered in the U.S. Patent and Trademark Office.

Printed in the United States of America

For information:
MULTNOMAH PUBLISHERS, INC.
POST OFFICE BOX 1720
SISTERS, OREGON 97759

Library of Congress Cataloging-in-Publication Data
Lists to live by : the fourth collection / compiled by Alice Gray, Steve Stephens, John Van Diest.
        p. cm.
      ISBN 1-59052-059-9 (Paperback)
          1-59052-435-7
    1. Conduct of life--Miscellanea. 2. Christian life--Miscellanea. I. Gray, Alice, 1939-
  II. Stephens, Steve. III. Van Diest, John,
      BJ1581.2 L554 2003
      646.7--dc21   2002013134

04 05 06 07 08—10 9 8 7 6 5 4

4

Lists
to live by

For Everything
That Really Matters

COMPILED BY

ALICE GRAY

STEVE STEPHENS

JOHN VAN DIEST

Multnomah® Publishers *Sisters, Oregon*

CONTENTS

INTRODUCTION
LISTS WILL CHANGE YOUR LIFE

THE LISTS IN THIS BOOK WILL...

- *Encourage you*
- *Inspire you*
- *Strengthen you*
- *Challenge you*
- *Inform you*
- *And change your life*

Over half a million people can't be wrong. Business professionals, parents, athletes, teenagers, pastors, and everyone who wants a better life are applauding the *Lists to Live By* books.

By popular request this bestselling series returns with a fourth collection of over 200 powerful and engaging lists. Topics include success, relationships, virtues, faith, parenting, and wisdom. Every list is a treasure—the best parts of a whole book presented on a single page.

It is a motivational tool, a reference volume, a discussion starter, and an enjoyable read all rolled into one. Pick up this collection and you might just be surprised at how it changes the way you live.

ALICE GRAY   STEVE STEPHENS   JOHN VAN DIEST

1
Success

Making the most of your life

SEVEN PRINCIPLES OF SUCCESS

1. It's okay to fail.

2. Don't be afraid to start.

3. Dare to dream big.

4. Don't be afraid to try something new.

5. Take things one step at a time.

6. Keep moving forward.

7. The only thing that can stop you is you.

PAT WILLIAMS
CONDENSED FROM "SECRETS FROM THE MOUNTAIN"

BARRIERS TO GROWTH

1. *I'm comfortable.*—Staying in the comfort zone and living at the present level of success is easier and less stressful than exerting effort to make needed changes.

2. *I'm afraid of failure.*—Fear of making a mistake or risking possible failure discourages trying anything new or different.

3. *Disapproval hurts.*—The desire to avoid disapproval, either by themselves or by others, limits many to behavior that is calculated to please.

4. *I don't want to rock the boat.*—Anxiety about changing the status quo convinces some that change is negative and not worth the risk.

5. *I don't have what it takes.*—A poverty mentality, coupled with a false sense of inferiority, causes some people to believe they do not deserve the rewards of using their full potential.

6. *Success might not be good for me.*—An illogical fear of success prevents many from breaking the success barrier. They feel unworthy or they fear they will not know how to handle success, so they subconsciously avoid it.

7. *God doesn't want me to succeed.*—This unfounded belief of God sends many great dreams into a tailspin. Scripture says, "I pray that you may prosper in all things and be in health, just as your soul prospers" (3 John 1:2, NKJV).

PAUL J. MEYER, FOUNDER OF SUCCESS MOTIVATION INTERNATIONAL
FROM "UNLOCKING YOUR LEGACY"

YOU AND YOUR BOSS

§

Respect your boss's authority.

§

Accept your boss's correction.

§

Encourage your boss.

§

Listen to your boss.

§

Ask your boss if you can do more.

§

Support your boss whenever possible.

§

Believe the best of your boss.

§

Pray for your boss.

STEVE MARR
ADAPTED FROM "BUSINESS PROVERBS"

TEN COMMANDMENTS OF SUCCESS

I. WORK HARD
Hard work is the best investment a person can make.

II. STUDY HARD
Knowledge enables us to work more intelligently and effectively.

III. HAVE INITIATIVE
Ruts often deepen into graves.

IV. LOVE YOUR WORK
Then you will find pleasure in mastering it.

}. BE EXACT
Slipshod methods bring slipshod results.

VI. HAVE THE SPIRIT OF CONQUEST
Thus you can successfully handle and overcome difficulties.

VII. CULTIVATE PERSONALITY
Personality is to a person what perfume is to a flower.

VIII. HELP AND SHARE WITH OTHERS
The real test of business greatness lies
in giving opportunity to others.

IX. BE DEMOCRATIC
Unless you feel right toward others, you
can never be a successful leader.

X. IN ALL THINGS, DO YOUR BEST
The person who has done less than their best has done nothing.

CHARLES MICHAEL SCHWAB
FIRST PRESIDENT OF U.S. STEEL

PRINCIPLES OF CRITICISM

1.
Never point out the errors without offering a solution.
The time for correction must also become a time to teach.

2.
Criticize the act, never the person.
People have emotions that need to be respected.

3.
Never condemn in public.
*Even if the error is minor, don't embarrass someone by
pointing out mistakes in front of colleagues.*

4.
Always end with praise.
*Some people believe you should start with a compliment and
end with correction. I reverse it—preferring to end on a positive note.*

NEIL ESKELIN
CONDENSED FROM "LEADING WITH LOVE"

WHAT KEEPS US FROM DREAMING

Overwhelmed by the now

Critical people

Fear of failure

Past failures

Laziness

Depression

Distraction

Lack of faith

Lack of resources

Lack of confidence

Don't know how to start

Don't know how to dream

DR. STEVE STEPHENS
PSYCHOLOGIST AND SEMINAR SPEAKER

BUSINESS PRINCIPLES

- Take care of small problems before they become big ones.

- Don't allow yourself to become dull on your job.

- Set a positive example.

- Learn to accept constructive criticism.

- Establish a clear vision and goals.

- Maintain a cheerful disposition and a confident, optimistic outlook.

- Speak the truth, even if the situation might be uncomfortable.

- Communicate your expectations clearly and completely.

- Learn from your mistakes.

- Move forward, or be prepared to be pushed back.

- Tackle the challenges you don't want to face first.

- Give genuine praise.

- Show tenacity in the face of adversity.

- Build teamwork and a climate of encouragement.

- Pledge yourself to continuous improvement.

- Focus your attention and energy.

- Establish a reputation for fairness and integrity.

- Learn, adapt, and grow in your job.

- Make and keep firm commitments.

- Set a standard for yourself that goes above and beyond

  expectations.

- Seek out experienced counsel and listen to it.

- Pay attention to the little things.

- Establish achievable benchmarks for each month, quarter,

  and year.

- Tackle the important priorities immediately.

STEVE MARR
ADAPTED FROM "BUSINESS PROVERBS"

Allow time in and time out.

Consistently effective people turn off the switch, put their feet up, and have deliberate time for relaxation.

Anticipate and prevent problems.

Think ahead and prepare for what might go wrong.

Avoid searching by having no temporary parking places.

When you acquire something, immediately assign it a regular parking place.

Carry and use a daily action sheet of some kind.

Use a Palm Pilot, a three-by-five-inch card in your pocket, a page with yellow sticky notes next to your calendar, or a list on the refrigerator. Have a written daily focus in hand and have a written weekly focus within reach.

Celebrate.

Whether it is kneeling and giving thanks, patting yourself on the back, or drawing a red line through an accomplishment listed on your daily action sheet—or all of the above—take the time to celebrate.

Divide big jobs into workable steps.

When you divide big jobs into steps you help yourself concentrate. You motivate yourself. You free yourself to accomplish one step at a time.

Do central and essential priorities now.

The secret is not just to do them first; it is to do them now.

Do it daily.

Daily faithful steps in the right direction beat occasional flashes of productivity.

Enjoy giving.

There is more happiness in giving than in receiving. The people who have the most energy for accomplishments and lifestyle are the ones who invest time volunteering.

Finish fully.
Complete as much as you can. Take a task to completion and get joy from crossing the finish line.

Group related activities.
If you have ever made a trip to a grocery store for one missing ingredient, you know the importance of grouping related items. If you are writing a letter, write a couple more. It is almost as easy to write three as one.

Help others get what they want.
This helps you have more energy and joy.

Plan frequently.
Planning prevents problems. Planning shows you where you can contribute to your objectives. Planning pays off for you and others.

Put a cushion in your calendar.
Allow some emergency time before a deadline.

Set and meet deadlines.
Deadlines energize and stimulate. They help you enjoy getting things done that would otherwise slide.

Track your time.
Know how long it takes to do everything.

Use timetables.
Timetables increase your productivity at the start of a project. They help you relax because you know when you are on schedule.

Work in cycles.
When you finish something, start preparing for the next event.

DRU SCOTT DECKER
ADAPTED FROM "FINDING MORE TIME IN YOUR LIFE"

- Love people, not programs.

- Nurture people by being flexible and dynamic.

- Establish a reputation for being gentle and kind.

- Constantly show your interest in others.

- Choose words people will embrace.

- Take the time to write down your values and beliefs.

- Patience produces lasting results.

- Adopt a personal code of ethics.

- Build on a foundation of truth.

- Offer a vision of hope.

- Love people for who they are.

- Discover the dreams of others.

- Offer people what they love.

- Express and demonstrate your gratitude.

- Treat people with admiration, courtesy, and respect.

- Don't be threatened by people with potential.

- To demonstrate trust, delegate.

- Create a nonintimidating atmosphere.

- Don't avoid unpleasant topics.

- Learn to truly understand others.

- Never betray a confidence.

- Become a passionate communicator.

- Don't be known as a critic.

- Emphasize what you have in common.

- Be quick to acknowledge your errors.

NEIL ESKELIN
CONDENSED FROM "LEADING WITH LOVE"

QUALITIES OF A GREAT MENTOR

Aware of their values

Growing in self-awareness

Always learning

Forward-looking

Realistically optimistic

Enthusiastic about change

Action-oriented

Flexible

Courageous enough to be forthright

Genuinely caring

Trustworthy and respected

GARY COLLINS
CONDENSED FROM "CHRISTIAN COACHING"

WHAT A MENTOR CAN HELP YOU DO

1. Develop skills in areas like athletics, music, money management, public speaking, parenting, or leadership.
2. Discover and develop passions.
3. Find a life purpose.
4. Build a clearer vision for the future.
5. Develop a mission statement.
6. Learn to manage change effectively.
7. Learn to relate to people effectively.
8. Find clear values.
9. Build communication skills.
10. Appraise performance.
11. Get out of ruts and move forward.
12. Learn to think and see things differently.
13. Expand the capacity to take action.
14. Get free of self-sabotaging behavior and destructive self-talk.
15. Build better teams.
16. Build self-confidence.
17. Find meaning in what one is doing.
18. Get the courage to take risks.
19. Learn to take responsibility.
20. Develop a closer walk with God.

GARY COLLINS
CONDENSED FROM "CHRISTIAN COACHING"

PERSONAL GOAL SETTING

1. SPIRITUAL GROWTH GOALS.
   This includes quiet times, journaling time, and prayer time.

2. FAMILY GROWTH GOALS.
   Family goals help me focus on being a better parent and a better husband.

3. LEADERSHIP GROWTH GOALS.
   For myself, I list 12 different books to read, one per month, and listen to a certain number of audiotapes.

4. PHYSICAL GROWTH GOALS.
   I'm aware that I need to eat right and exercise to stay healthy and keep my mind focused.

5. PROFESSIONAL GROWTH GOALS.
   These goals might involve studying communication or maybe taking a computer class or a graphics class.

6. PERSONAL GROWTH GOALS.
   Scheduling vacation time, taking a day off, looking for someone to build into and mentor me—these are all areas in which I strive to stay focused and grow personally.

CRAIG JUTILA
CONDENSED FROM "LEADERSHIP ESSENTIALS FOR CHILDREN'S MINISTRY"

HOW TO FIND YOUR PASSION

§

Ask someone who knows you well to identify your passions.

§

Think of times in your life when you felt exuberant and
excited to be alive. What might this say about your passion?

§

When you were young and your parents could not find you,
what did they assume you were doing? What does
this say about your passion?

§

If you had no limitations in terms of money or time,
what would you do?

§

Look at your environment.
Does this reveal what really interests and excites you?

§

Pray that God will reveal His passion for your life.

GARY COLLINS
CONDENSED FROM "CHRISTIAN COACHING"

WE ARE IMPACTED MOST BY...

...people of courage.

...people of character.

...people of discipline.

...people of excellence.

...people of compassion.

...people of encouragement.

...people of vision.

...people of generosity.

...people of wisdom.

...people of faith.

DR. STEVE STEPHENS
PSYCHOLOGIST AND SEMINAR SPEAKER

THE SUCCESSFUL PERSON

- Sets priorities

- Says no if she needs to

- Laughs at his own mistakes

- Has control of her emotions

- Dresses up for special occasions

- Completes his work in a timely fashion

- Refrains from embarrassing behavior

- Wears attractive clothing in public

- Follows a weekly exercise program

- Sends appreciation notes

- Works toward becoming organized

- Chooses encouraging friends

- Uses words that affirm

- Controls her body weight

- Learns from his failures

- Sees her own successes

GLENDA HOTTON, M.A.
COUNSELOR FOR WOMEN

1. **But there's nothing I can do.**
   You may not always be able to do everything you would like to do or need to do, but you can certainly take some steps. A small step in the right direction is much better than waiting until you can do everything.

2. **It doesn't work for me.**
   Time techniques are only tools; they can help make our work easier, but they can't do the job by themselves. Their degree of usefulness depends on the skill with which we use them. We sharpen our skills when we use them again and again.

3. **But I've already taken the course or read the book.**
   Read books. Take courses. Listen to tapes. And talk with people. Keep yourself well supplied with ideas and inspiration. It's one of the best ways to stay on target with your time.

4. **I just can't get organized around here.**
   Don't let an imperfect situation be an excuse to do nothing about your own time problems. Resentment about the disorganization around you is a waste of your time. Take the initiative. Work on improving your own time use. Do what you can, regardless of less than ideal circumstances.

5. **I can't get organized because people keep interrupting me.**
   Interruptions are an inevitable part of everyday living. Don't waste time waiting for them to disappear. Learn how to handle them instead.

6. **I need someone to motivate me.**
   This myth is based on the common belief that someone or something outside ourselves controls our feelings. The reality is that we are all in charge of our own feelings. You don't have to wait for anyone else to inspire you. You can become your own inspiration.

7. **I'm waiting until I have more time.**
   This is a very common myth. Consider it logically and you'll realize it doesn't hold up. Putting off doing what counts most to you now until you have "more time" is like saying you can't go on a diet until you lose some weight.

DRU SCOTT DECKER
CONDENSED FROM "FINDING MORE TIME IN YOUR LIFE"

HIGHLIGHT
Always keep a highlighter with you and mark meaningful quotes or impacting principles.

WRITE
Record the most important ideas in your journal and review them from time to time.

ASK
Read actively by asking yourself questions like, *What is the author's purpose in writing this book? What's the key idea of the book? How can this book help me in my life?*

THINK
Ponder what you read. As one old sage said, "It is better to master 10 books than just read 1,000."

SPEAK
Share with a friend some of the principles you've learned and how they have affected your life.

KYLE LIEDTKE
MEDIA CONSULTANT

SEVEN WAYS TO GAIN INFLUENCE

1. CLEAR VISION
People will follow you only if they know where you're going.
People follow a leader who gives clear direction.

2. CREDIBILITY
Live what you teach. Keep your promises. Be trustworthy.

3. CONFIDENCE
People want to follow a leader who has confidence.

4. CHARACTER
Dwight L. Moody said, "Character is what you do in the dark."
Don't be tempted to meet legitimate needs in illegitimate ways.

5. COURAGE
Leaders will be tested. You can count on obstacles in your pathway
as you lead from where you are to where you need to go.

6. COMMITMENT
If you are to succeed as a leader, you must be more committed than
anyone else.

7. CARE
Everyone wants to know, "Does the leader care about me?"
Showing your love is as simple as spending time
to build one-on-one relationships with them.

DALE GALLOWAY
ADAPTED FROM "ON-PURPOSE LEADERSHIP"

2
Day by Day

Growing better and stronger

THINGS TO DO EVERY DAY

§ Appreciate the people around you.

§ Forgive all who ask.

§ Stand up for those less fortunate than you.

§ Work hard.

§ Have patience with people.

§ Fight evil.

§ Let go of grudges.

§ Stay true to your word.

§ Laugh at yourself.

§ Move out of your comfort zone.

§ Revel in fresh ideas.

§ Do something that will last beyond your lifetime.

DR. STEVE STEPHENS
PSYCHOLOGIST AND SEMINAR SPEAKER

TIPS FOR LIFE

1. Give people more than they expect, and do so cheerfully.

2. Don't believe all you hear, spend all you have, or sleep all you'd like.

3. Don't say, "I love you" unless you really mean it.

4. When you say, "I'm sorry," look the person in the eye.

5. Be engaged at least six months before you get married.

6. Love deeply and passionately. You might get hurt, but it's the only way to live life completely.

7. In disagreements, fight fair. No name-calling.

8. Don't judge people by their relatives.

9. When someone asks you a question you don't want to answer, smile and ask, "Why do you want to know?"

10. Call your mom.

11. Say, "Bless you" when you hear someone sneeze.

12. Don't let a little squabble damage a good friendship.

13. When you realize you've made a mistake, take immediate steps to correct it.

14. Smile when picking up the phone. The caller will hear it in your voice.

15. Marry someone you love to talk to. As you get older, good conversation will be one of the principal elements of an enduring relationship.

16. Remember that silence is sometimes the best answer.

17. Read more books and watch less TV.

18. In disagreements with loved ones, deal with the current situation. Don't bring up the past.

19. Never interrupt when you are being flattered.

20. Mind your own business.

21. Trust in God, but lock your car.

FROM "DEAR ANN LANDERS"
SYNDICATED COLUMN

ESSENTIALS OF HAPPINESS

Something to do

Something to love

Something to hope for

JOSEPH ADDISON
POET AND ESSAYIST

THE BEST THINGS IN LIFE ARE NEAREST

Breath in your nostrils,

light in your eyes,

flowers at your feet,

duties at your hand,

and the path of right just before you.

ROBERT LOUIS STEVENSON
NOVELIST AND TRAVELER

WATCH YOUR ATTITUDE

∽ Remember that you can miss a lot of good things in life by having the wrong attitude.

∽ Become the most positive and enthusiastic person you know.

∽ Forgive quickly.

∽ Spend your life lifting people up, not putting people down.

∽ Make the most of the best and the least of the worst.

∽ Be cheerful, even when you don't feel like it.

∽ Be happy with what you have while working for what you want.

∽ Look for the opportunity that's hidden in every adversity.

∽ Don't expect life to be fair.

∽ Never underestimate the power of laughter.

∽ Count your blessings.

∽ Remember that if you look for the worst in life and in people, you'll find it. But if you look for the best, you'll find that instead.

H. JACKSON BROWN JR. AND ROCHELLE PENNINGTON
CONDENSED FROM "HIGHLIGHTED IN YELLOW"

40 OFTEN OVERLOOKED BLESSINGS

1. Answered prayers. 2. Expressions of unconditional love and support. 3. Your health. 4. The aroma of something delicious wafting from the kitchen. 5. An afternoon to do as you please. 6. Holding your child in your arms. 7. Delighting in other people's children. 8. Witnessing the birth of new life. 9. The fragrance of a vacation day. 10. Trying something new and loving it. 11. Two hours in a wonderful bookstore. 12. A nap. 13. Realizing that there are no coincidences. 14. The sacred release of a good cry. 15. The loyal, loving companionship of pets. 16. Finding a parking space exactly when you need one. 17. Summoning up the courage to surmount a challenge. 18. Meeting a deadline. 19. Reading a book that changes your life. 20. Receiving flowers. 21. Letting go gracefully without regrets. 22. A miracle. 23. Bargains at thrift shops, flea markets, garage sales. 24. The sense of relief throwing stuff out brings. 25. Your mentor. 26. The long awaited phone call with good news. 27. When the repair bill is less than you'd expected. 28. A sense of humor during good and rough patches. 29. Not losing your temper. 30. Perfect timing. 31. Fitting into last year's clothes. 32. Sharing your aspirations for the future with a close friend. 33. Pampering yourself. 34. The generosity and hospitality of good neighbors. 35. Rediscovering old family photos. 36. Playing hooky. 37. An unexpected compliment that makes your day. 38. Completing the crossword puzzle without help. 39. Paying off your credit card balance. 40. The sound of raindrops on your roof at night.

SARAH BAN BREATHNACH
CONDENSED FROM "THE SIMPLE ABUNDANCE JOURNAL OF GRATITUDE"

EIGHT REQUISITES
FOR CONTENTED LIVING

1.
Health enough to make work a pleasure;

2.
Wealth enough to support your needs;

3.
Strength enough to battle with difficulties and overcome them;

4.
Patience enough to toil until some good is accomplished;

5.
Charity enough to see some good in your neighbor;

6.
Love enough to move you to be useful and helpful to others;

7.
Faith enough to make real the things of God;

8.
Hope enough to remove all anxious fears concerning the future.

GOETHE
POET, PLAYWRIGHT, AND NOVELIST

SIMPLICITY...

§

eases our stress.

§

cleans away our clutter.

§

increases our appreciation.

§

clarifies our priorities.

§

purifies our heart.

§

uplifts our spirit.

§

settles our emotions.

§

encourages our friends.

§

deepens our peace.

§

builds our character.

DR. STEVE STEPHENS
PSYCHOLOGIST AND SEMINAR SPEAKER

SIDE EFFECTS OF WORRYING

Self-Doubt

It is a downward spiral that focuses on the negative and why things cannot be done versus why things can be done. It is a sinkhole, a debilitating attitude, and a terrible habit.

Mediocrity

Capable people who worry are rendered incapable of accomplishing their intended goal. Worry makes you peck around on the ground like a chicken when you were intended to soar like an eagle.

Fright

People who worry are not being cautious or thinking things over; they are simply scared. Running scared is the enemy of success, peace, contentment, happiness, joy, laughter, etc.

No Spark

The excitement is gone. Worry lets the air out of all you do, draining the fun and excitement from everything.

No Creativity

The freedom to be creative is squelched by worry. You simply cannot excel to your full potential when worry controls your thoughts.

Improper Shaping
You are molded and shaped by your thinking, and worries should not shape your future.

Hazy Results
Those who worry are second-guessing themselves, which produces a hesitancy that brings with it an unclear focus. Such a hazy goal will produce a hazy result.

Bad Habits
Worrying is a habit, the result of preconditioning and years of practice. The destructive habit of worrying turns people into prisoners.

Physical Ailments
The body reacts adversely to internal worries. John Haggai insightfully stated, "A distraught mind inevitably leads to a deteriorated body."

Wasted Time
Over 90 percent of what you worry about never comes to pass. To worry is to waste time; therefore, the more you worry, the less you accomplish.

PAUL J. MEYER
FROM "UNLOCKING YOUR LEGACY"

WHEN IT'S HARD TO GET UP...

STRETCH.
That gets the body going.

SMILE.
That puts the soul in the right attitude.

SAY, "GOD LOVES ME."
That sets the spirit right.

DR. RAY STEDMAN
FROM "THREEFOLD TECHNIQUE FOR A GREAT MORNING"

TAKE NOTHING FOR GRANTED...

For every right that you cherish,
you have a duty that you must fulfill.

For every hope that you entertain,
you have a task that you must perform.

For every good that you wish to preserve,
you will have to sacrifice your comfort and your ease.

There is nothing for nothing any longer.

GEORGE WASHINGTON
FIRST PRESIDENT OF THE UNITED STATES

TEN HABITS
TO MEMORIZE AND LIVE BY

1. Pick it up, don't pass it up; and don't put it down unless you put it away.

2. Finish what you start.

3. When you're on the telephone, visiting, or watching TV, do something productive with your hands.

4. If you can't talk and do something productive with your hands at the same time, put masking tape on your mouth and get your work done.

5. Eat sitting down.

6. Make your bed for your own self-respect.

7. Make sure that each room in the house serves its own purpose.

8. Do it when you think of it.

9. Don't write long letters.

10. Work faster; say no when you should and say yes when you can. Ask yourself, "If I do this, in a year from now, will it matter that I did it?"

PAM YOUNG AND PEGGY JONES
FROM "GET YOUR ACT TOGETHER"

ENRICH YOUR LIFE

> *Try making two small changes every day.*
> Take a different street, try a new restaurant, change your toothpaste, smile at someone you don't know, eat dessert first. There's a lot of landscape to explore off the beaten path.

> *Clear the clutter.*
> Take a good look at where you spend your time, and start with the obvious things: dead plants, old newspapers, and the like. You can rearrange every room in your house, but you don't have to. At least have a go at reorganizing your underwear drawer.

> *Rediscover the simple pleasures.*
> Do your possessions energize you, or are they a drain? If you're a habitual television watcher and want to discover more simple pleasures this week, try a TV-fast. Time will open up.

> *Realize not everything needs to be done today.*
> Prioritize based on what feels right, not just what your to-do list says. If the day's rhythm favors cleaning rather than returning phone calls, that's what should get done. Tasks will still get taken care of, but the result will be more creative and elegant. And you'll surely feel more peaceful.

JOAN BORYSENKO, PH.D.
FROM "INNER PEACE FOR BUSY PEOPLE"

TEN LIFE-DEFINING MOMENTS

1. WHEN CALLED TO OBEY

2. WHEN SEEKING TO BE KNOWN

3. WHEN FACED WITH FAILURE

4. WHEN PURSUING YOUR PURPOSE

5. WHEN TAKING A STAND

6. WHEN ENGAGED IN SUFFERING

7. WHEN ASKED TO FORGIVE

8. WHEN EXPERIENCING TEMPTATION

9. WHEN NEEDING TO REPENT

10. WHEN DECIDING ON GOD

JAMES EMERY WHITE
FROM "LIFE-DEFINING MOMENTS"

TAKE TIME FOR SILENCE

Sanctuary: Find a place free from distraction.

Invite new thoughts and the voice of God.

Listen and learn.

Evaluate emotions, ideas, dreams, convictions, and resolutions.

Never rush.

Confront challenging ideas.

Ease back into your world with a plan of action.

CURTIS TUCKER
PASTOR

THE SIMPLEST PLEASURES OF LIFE

§ Get up early enough to enjoy the wonder of a sunrise in leisure.

§ Find a bench at the nearest park. Enjoy an entire thermos of coffee without interruption.

§ Notice the intricate beauty of spiderwebs, pinecones, or icicles.

§ Sit on the porch, lean back, and watch the clouds reshape themselves until something identifiable emerges.

§ Meet a friend for a relaxed after-dinner conversation.

§ Spend 15 minutes simply concentrating on the sounds you hear outside in your own backyard.

§ Look at and smell every vegetable and piece of fruit you pick up before you put it in your shopping basket.

§ Count the shades of green (or blue, or red) you can see from your kitchen or office window.

§ Bake a dessert just to enjoy the aroma, then deliver it to someone who won't expect it.

LAVERNA KLIPPENSTEIN
ADAPTED FROM AN ARTICLE IN "CHRISTIAN LIVING" MAGAZINE

TEN UNCOMMON DELIGHTS

1.

The beauty of nature

2.

The miracle of a newborn

3.

The joy of discovery

4.

The awesomeness of God

5.

The thrill of accomplishment

6.

The passion of love

7.

The power of music

8.

The deliciousness of food

9.

The appreciation of life

10.

The surprise of a gift

DR. STEVE STEPHENS
PSYCHOLOGIST AND SEMINAR SPEAKER

DAY BY DAY

3
Relationships

Deepening your love for others

LOVE IS...

- ❦ asking about someone's day and truly caring about the answer.

- ❦ being patient, even when you're tired—*especially* when you're tired.

- ❦ writing a note of encouragement.

- ❦ buying someone flowers for no reason.

- ❦ caring—even when it's hard and you don't feel like it.

- ❦ trusting in someone when you're scared.

- ❦ saying you're sorry when you are wrong.

- ❦ praying for someone.

- ❦ forgiving someone again and again.

- ❦ providing a shoulder to cry on.

- ❦ holding your tongue.

- ❦ what God does for us.

DANAE JACOBSON, AGE 16
SELECTED FROM "THINGS I'VE LEARNED LATELY"

TEN WAYS TO CELEBRATE FRIENDSHIP

1. **Dump the guilt.**

   If people realize friendship is going to make them better parents, better spouses, more fulfilled and happier, then maybe they'll feel more justified in making friendship the priority it should be.

2. **Focus on real friends.**

   Decide who among your circle are authentic friends, rather than acquaintances, and concentrate on those connections.

3. **Plan brief get-togethers.**

   Issue invitations to friends for short visits with very specific time parameters.

4. **Don't limit it to lunch.**

   Does a hectic work schedule make lunch with a pal impossible? Try meeting for afternoon coffee or breakfast before the day's craziness sets in.

5. **Make it a habit.**

   The best way to find time for friendship is to create traditions. Create a routine, something you can count on that you don't have to negotiate.

6. **Sign up with a buddy.**

    Ensure that you and a pal hook up regularly by committing to an activity you both enjoy.

7. **Volunteer together.**

    Do you and a close friend champion a similar cause? Consider seeking volunteer work to share. Striving together for a worthwhile goal will undoubtedly deepen your friendship.

8. **Zap an e-mail.**

    E-mail provides a time-efficient way to keep in touch, allowing you to dispatch brief but meaningful messages. It doesn't replace the personal connection, but it helps keep the relationship alive when you're pressed for time.

9. **Talk while tackling a task.**

    Facing a boring chore? Cordless and cellular phones are available with headsets that allow both hands to remain free—ideal for dishing up your latest news while doing other jobs.

10. **If all else fails…just make time.**

    If you find your days consumed with the pursuit of money or a spotless home, take a deep breath and let some things go. Remember that the relationships we build are life's true treasures.

CATHERINE STIER
ADAPTED FROM "WOMAN'S DAY" MAGAZINE

TRUST BUSTERS   TRUST BUILDERS

TRUST BUSTERS	TRUST BUILDERS
1. Keeping secrets	1. Giving genuine praise in public
2. Talking behind people's backs	2. Keeping your word
3. Ignoring or minimizing people's feelings	3. Showing respect and courtesy
4. Placing things above people	4. Listening carefully
5. Breaking promises	5. Being dependable
6. Twisting the truth	6. Remembering special occasions
7. Being judgmental or critical	7. Speaking the truth in love
8. Hurting others intentionally	8. Supporting other's dreams
9. Taking care of personal needs and wants at the expense of others	9. Enjoying time together

DR. CAROL CLIFTON, PH.D.
PSYCHOLOGIST

SHOWING LOVE

Listening when you are speaking

Offering my help when you need it

Valuing all the wonderful things you do

Encouraging you when times are tough

TAMI STEPHENS
LOVING WIFE, LOVING MOTHER, LOVING FRIEND

RELATIONSHIPS

WHEN YOU'RE FEELING LONELY

Know you're not alone.
Not alone in feeling lonely, that is. Concentrating on helping someone else out of a lonely time can be a good loneliness-reducer.

Call an old friend.
When you're hungering for a friend, dialing up a pal from the past is such a treat that you'll hardly notice the long-distance tab.

Make the first move.
Don't sit back and wait for someone else to do it.

Take a risk.
Don't let past hurts—betrayal, a loss, or some other painful situation—keep you from making new friends. Good friends are worth the risk.

Remember past friendships.
It's healthy to reminisce. Thumb through letters from friends, photos, cards, scrapbooks, even yearbooks. Remembering when you were loved in the past is an encouraging reminder that you'll be loved again.

Grab a friendship minute.

When your schedule has squeezed out friendships, little chats can keep you going until you have the time for some deeper connections.

Be wary of Internet relationships.

If you have an e-friendship, make sure it's with someone you already know personally. Friends you "meet" on the Internet can too easily misrepresent themselves. Be cautious.

Keep on looking.

If you're friendless because there isn't a person who seems "just right" for the job, hang on to hope and stay on the lookout for a friend. You may need to look at those you know with a less critical eye.

RHONDA RHEA
CONDENSED FROM "TODAY'S CHRISTIAN WOMAN" MAGAZINE

A CARING PERSON HAS...

hands to help others.

feet to hasten them to the poor and needy.

eyes to see misery and want.

ears to hear the sighs and sorrows of men.

AUGUSTINE OF HIPPO
THEOLOGIAN

FRIENDSHIP CHECKUP

§

Do I seek to bring out the best in others,
even if it means they will outshine me?

§

Do I do unto others as I would have done unto me?

§

Do I keep confidences?

§

Do I promote unity and win-win outcomes?

§

Do I try to reciprocate when loyalty, favors, and
appreciation are given to me?

§

Do I desire to create opportunities
rather than obstacles for others?

PAM FARREL
FROM "WOMAN OF CONFIDENCE"

HOW TO HANDLE CRITICISM

1.

LISTEN.

Don't begin planning your defense while they are still talking. Take a deep breath and try to stay calm until they are finished.

2.

AVOID RETALIATION.

No matter how harsh or unjustified a person may come across, control your emotions. If you get angry it will only escalate the situation and cause further turmoil. The Bible says that a gentle answer turns away wrath.

3.

DON'T RESPOND IMMEDIATELY.

Say you will consider what has been said and that you will get back to them in a day or two. And then do it!

4.

RESPECT THE CRITICISM.

Even if the criticism seems unfair, there may be some truth to it. Look at criticism as an opportunity to become a better person, worker, friend, or family member.

5.

BE HONEST WITH YOURSELF.

Consider what was said, focus on the truth, and make a plan to change what you can.

6.

FORGIVE.

If they were abrasive in their approach, forgive them and don't hold it against them in the future.

7.

HAVE A GOOD ATTITUDE.

Even if you think the criticism was undeserved or severe, thank the person for communicating their concerns to you. Remember that every situation in life will make you either bitter or better—it's your choice.

KYLE LIEDTKE
MEDIA CONSULTANT

THE FOUR-WAY TEST
OF THINGS WE THINK, SAY, AND DO

1.

Is it the TRUTH?

2.

Is it FAIR to all concerned?

3.

Will it build GOODWILL and BETTER FRIENDSHIPS?

4.

Will it be BENEFICIAL to all concerned?

HERBERT J. TAYLOR
ROTARY INTERNATIONAL PRESIDENT, 1954–1955

SEVEN STEPS THAT LEAD TO PROBLEMS

1.
An inability to forgive little things.

2.
A tendency to hold grudges.

3.
An undisciplined thought life.

4.
A refusal to say "I'm sorry."

5.
An insensitivity to the other's feelings.

6.
A refusal to try seeing situations from the other's point of view.

7.
An inflexible spirit.

JACK AND CAROLE MAYHALL
CONDENSED FROM "DISCIPLESHIP JOURNAL" MAGAZINE

WHEN SOMEONE HURTS YOUR FEELINGS

Reason with yourself.

Reveal your heart.

Remember that you have also hurt others.

Resist holding onto the hurt.

Release the one who hurt you.

Reach out for help.

Restore your smile.

Reconcile the relationship, if at all possible.

Refocus your life on what is positive.

Reflect on what you have just learned.

MARK BELOKONNY
PASTOR AND TEACHER

HOW TO SHOW RESPECT

- Look at a person's face when talking or listening to them.

- Show up at events on time.

- Say "please" and "thank you" and "excuse me" as needed.

- Speak kindly.

- Let them go first.

- Apologize when you offend others.

- Don't crowd people's space.

- Wait patiently.

- Keep your promises

- Take people's requests seriously.

- Leave things better than how you found them.

- Be mindful of other's property and privacy.

TAMI STEPHENS
MOTHER OF THREE

SLOW & QUICK

SLOW TO REACT…
quick to listen.

SLOW TO QUESTION…
quick to believe.

SLOW TO CONDEMN…
quick to defend.

SLOW TO BOAST…
quick to compliment.

SLOW TO DEMAND…
quick to give.

SLOW TO CRITICIZE…
quick to encourage.

SLOW TO RESENT…
quick to forgive.

SLOW TO GIVE UP…
quick to hope.

COLLECTED FROM EIGHT COUPLES WHO CHOOSE TO LOVE

WHAT GOOD FRIENDS DO

1.
Show concern for each others' happiness.

2.
Look forward to spending time together.

3.
Celebrate their joys and weep with their sorrows.

4.
Grant space if the other needs it.

5.
Know one another's weaknesses and don't point them out.

6.
Praise one another's strengths.

7.
Share their hearts with honesty and sensitivity.

8.
Demonstrate trustworthiness.

9.
Believe the best in each other.

10.
Pray regularly for their friends and families.

ALICE GRAY, DR. STEVE STEPHENS, AND JOHN VAN DIEST

WITHOUT LOVE...

All I say is ineffective.

All I know is incomplete.

All I believe is insufficient.

All I give is insignificant.

All I accomplish is inadequate.

MARK BELOKONNY, PASTOR AND TEACHER
ADAPTED FROM 1 CORINTHIANS 13:1-3

KEYS TO KINDNESS

1. Treat everyone you meet like you want to be treated.

2. Make it a habit to do nice things for people who'll never find out.

3. Be kinder than necessary.

4. Be open and accessible. The next person you meet could become your best friend.

5. Never underestimate the power of a kind word or deed.

6. Seek out the good in people.

7. Never allow a friend to grieve alone.

8. Be there when people need you.

9. Practice empathy. Try to see things from other people's points of view.

10. Look for opportunities to make people feel important.

11. When you receive a kindness, pass it on.

12. Be the first to say hello.

H. JACKSON BROWN JR. AND ROCHELLE PENNINGTON
CONDENSED FROM "HIGHLIGHTED IN YELLOW"

TOGETHER

Walk along the beach together.

Read a great book together.

Enjoy a sunset together.

Laugh until it hurts together.

Listen to romantic music together.

Snuggle in front of a fire together.

Watch your favorite movie together.

Cook a meal together.

Help someone in need together.

Build wonderful memories together.

DR. STEVE STEPHENS
PSYCHOLOGIST AND SEMINAR SPEAKER

4
Marriage
Building lifelong togetherness

RULES FOR MARRIAGE

Be a team.

Be supportive.

Say what you mean, but don't say it meanly.

Don't use the D word (divorce).

Don't ask your single friends for marital advice.

Have a family dinner at least once a week.

Do things you don't want to do.

Don't try to do it all.

Don't expect applause for doing chores.

Don't nag.

ELLEN FEIN AND SHERRI SCHNEIDER
CONDENSED FROM "THE RULES FOR MARRIAGE"

IS YOUR MARRIAGE A COVENANT OR A CONTRACT?

A CONTRACT IS AN AGREEMENT MADE IN DISTRUST.
A covenant is an agreement made in trust.

A CONTRACT IS CONDITIONAL IN NATURE.
A covenant is unconditional in nature.

A CONTRACT FOCUSES ON THE GROWTH OF SELF.
A covenant focuses on the giving of self.

A CONTRACT IS PREDICATED ON RESULTS.
A covenant is predicated on relationships.

A CONTRACT IS MADE AT ARM'S LENGTH.
A covenant is made at arm's embrace.

A CONTRACT ASKS, "WHAT AM I GETTING FROM THIS MARRIAGE?"
A covenant asks, "What am I bringing to this marriage?"

A CONTRACT IS ENFORCED BY A COURT.
A covenant is enforced by character.

A CONTRACT IS BOUND BY LEGALISM AND LEVERAGE.
A covenant is bound by love and loyalty.

A CONTRACT IS CONVENIENCE-BASED.
A covenant is commitment-based.

A CONTRACT IS A "HAVE-TO" COMMITMENT.
A covenant is a "want-to" commitment.

A CONTRACT IS FOR A SPECIFIED PERIOD OF TIME.
A covenant is forever.

IN A CONTRACT NOBODY LEAVES UNTIL THE TERMS ARE MET.
In a covenant nobody leaves—period!

FRED LOWERY
CONDENSED FROM "COVENANT MARRIAGE"

TEN WAYS TO SHOW YOUR HUSBAND RESPECT

1. Ask for his opinion.
2. Tell others where he excels.
3. Listen to his ideas.
4. Prepare his favorite meal.
5. Don't mother him.
6. Encourage his interests.
7. Give him time to be alone.
8. Say "thank you" often.
9. Respond to his touch.
10. Let him be himself.

TEN WAYS TO SHOW YOUR WIFE HONOR

1. Praise her publicly.
2. Say "thank you" often.
3. Open doors for her.
4. Wait on her joyfully.
5. Wait on her patiently.
6. Seek her opinion.
7. Take her advice.
8. Respect her feelings.
9. Bring her a gift.
10. Listen, listen, listen.

H. DALE BURKE
ADAPTED FROM "DIFFERENT BY DESIGN"

SEVEN LOVES OF MARRIAGE

An enduring love...that rides the rolling waves like a sailboat, drawing strength from the shifting winds.

An exploring love...that keeps us holding hands with excitement and a sense of adventure as we anticipate the next bend in the road.

An attentive love...that reminds us that the life we desire together is fragile and needs sunlight, water, and daily care.

A sharing love...in which we've seen that the view from the bridge between us is a wider, grander sight than we could have ever seen from either shore.

A spontaneous love...that embraces each new day with wide-open eyes and refuses to allow the pale and diminished expectations of others to dilute our joy.

A sheltering love...that protects our investment in one another from all that would erode its commitment or quench its flame.

A beacon of love...that unites us in a life purpose bigger than ourselves, bigger than our marriage, bigger than the whole world.

~~~

THOMAS AND NANETTE KINKADE
CONDENSED FROM "THE MANY LOVES OF MARRIAGE"

MARRIAGE

ROMANTIC TIPS FOR TRAVELERS

Always hold hands.

Kiss at stop lights and stop signs.

Don't argue or complain.

Don't fight over the map.

If you get lost, make it an adventure.

Each time you see a bird, tell your spouse how he makes your heart soar.

Say "I love you" at railroad crossings.

Squeeze your spouse in tunnels and on bridges.

Take turns sharing one thing
you appreciate about each other at every ten-mile marker.

Make others think you're newlyweds.

GEORGE AND VALERIE STUART
NEWLYWEDS FOR 12 YEARS

SEVEN WAYS
TO FLIRT WITH YOUR SPOUSE

1. **Write a love story** about how you met and get it printed and bound.

2. **Whisper something romantic** to your spouse in a crowded room.

3. **Mail a love letter** to your spouse at work.

4. **Sketch your dream house together** and talk about the possibilities for each room.

5. **Put on your spouse's favorite romantic music** and take her dancing around your candlelit living room.

6. **Remember to look into your spouse's eyes** when he tells you about his day.

7. **Snuggle together** on the sofa and reminisce through old photo albums.

DOUG FIELDS
FROM "100 FUN AND FABULOUS WAYS TO FLIRT WITH YOUR SPOUSE"

EVERY HUSBAND SHOULD ASK HIS WIFE...

EVERY WIFE SHOULD ASK HER HUSBAND...

• Do you know that I truly love you, and do I make it obvious? If not, what can I do to improve that?

• Do you feel that I express my love to you enough in front of the children so there's no question in their mind of my love for you? If not, how can I improve it?

• Am I treating you as the most important person on earth to me? What could increase that feeling in you?

• I promised to cherish you. Do you feel that way, and what could I do to strengthen that?

• What is your greatest concern about our family, and have you felt free to express it to me? If you've expressed it, have I listened?

• Do you feel that I'm helping you fulfill your God-given potential? How can I improve that?

• Am I doing anything that would ever lead you to be tempted to compromise in any area? If so, what could I do to change?

• Would you tell me your most significant dreams about the future?

• Am I doing enough to make you feel adequate in our relationship and assuring you that I see you that way?

• I know it's important for you to feel honored and affirmed. Do I make you feel that way, and what can I do to improve?

• How can I help you best succeed at your work as you provide for the needs of our family?

• Do you feel that I know and understand what your greatest dreams are for the future?

• What could I do to better support your leadership in our family?

• Am I doing anything that would ever lead you to be tempted to compromise in any area? If so, what could I do to change?

BOB RECCORD
FROM "BENEATH THE SURFACE"

CREATE QUALITY TIME

∞ START IT NOW.

Create your own special evenings. If you have kids, put them in bed early, build a fire, prepare some snacks, and spend an hour or two together—without the television or telephone to distract you.

∞ GET TOGETHER.

When you go out, don't always pick movies or dinners with friends where your one-on-one time will be limited. Go to a coffee shop or bookstore and talk—about anything.

∞ MELT ANGER.

If something is bothering you, don't get into the bed, yank at the covers, and hug your side of the bed. Try to talk about it in a calm manner. If you do go to bed angry, try to understand why you are angry and agree to talk later.

∞ MAKE MINUTES COUNT.

Think about those five-minute segments that sometimes comprise all of the communication you have with your spouse. Do you make the most of them? Are the five minutes spent in a meaningful way or not?

KAY COLES JAMES
ADAPTED FROM "WHAT I WISH I'D KNOWN BEFORE I GOT MARRIED"

MARRIAGE

1. *Mark your calendar with a specific time.* You must set this up just like a business or dentist appointment.

2. *Make one day a week your calendar time.* This is a time when you plan your together times for the week. It can be simply ten to fifteen minutes to arrange calendars, but it is where you *write down* when you will connect during the coming week.

3. *Plan different types of time.* There needs to be time simply talking about our days, time for conflict resolution, and *fun only* times (dates, cuddles, walks) that we protect from any type of conflict.

4. *Implement a set of rules like the Three B's.* The kids can only interrupt if someone is *bleeding,* someone is *broken,* or something is *burning.*

5. *Find a specific place.* Bedrooms can be a good place to talk but I encourage you not to let the bedroom become a place of conflict resolution; it should be a place of intimate connecting. The symbolism is important.

6. *Establish goals.* Answer, "Why do we want to spend time together?" From that, you realize that you really do want the same thing—a fun, emotionally intimate marriage.

7. ***Protect, protect, protect.*** Too many clients leave my office vowing to spend time (at least three thirty-minute couple times over the next week) only to return seven days later without having done it once. They let other things invade. Instead of training to run, they ate Twinkies.

8. ***Drop defensiveness.*** Couples in conflict are more prone to interpret their mate's comments and actions in a negative way, even when their mate meant them as neutral or even positive. Believe the best about your partner; remember, you both want the same thing—a good marriage.

9. ***Be realistic.*** Saying you will spend time together seven days a week will frustrate you and eventually cause you to give up. There should be a brief "how are you?" connection every day, but as far as carving out twenty to thirty minutes to share your heart, three to four days a week is more realistic.

10. ***Don't give up.*** Keep working to make it happen. A marathoner has to get over the soreness and get into a routine, but once established, it is easier to keep the training going.

DR. TIM ALAN GARDNER
FROM "MARRIAGE PARTNERSHIP" MAGAZINE

DON'TS OF MARRIAGE

DON'T be angry at the same time.

DON'T yell at each other unless the house is on fire.

DON'T resist yielding to the wishes of the other.

DON'T criticize unlovingly.

DON'T bring up mistakes of the past.

DON'T let the day end without giving your spouse at least one compliment.

DON'T meet without an affectionate welcome.

DON'T let the sun go down on an unresolved argument.

DON'T hold on to pride—ask for forgiveness.

DON'T forget it takes two to make a quarrel but only one to stop it.

GLENDA HOTTON, M.A.
COUNSELOR

DO'S OF MARRIAGE

§ Verbally share the events of the day.

§ Renew statements regarding the relationship: "I love you." "You are special to me." "I missed you." "I have been looking forward to being with you."

§ Touch each other in meaningful ways—hugs, kisses, holding hands, sitting close.

§ Remember, commitment leads to communication; communication stimulates forgiveness; and forgiveness offers grace, which develops intimacy.

§ Show appreciation for something your partner has done— say "thank you."

§ Take turns asking and explaining when you have misunderstood one another.

§ Share hopes and dreams—a basic key to a close relationship.

§ Be a good listener—no response may be necessary.

GLENDA HOTTON, M.A.
COUNSELOR

HOW TO LISTEN

Lean forward and look into her eyes.

Inquire by saying, "Tell me more."

Stop interrupting with your "answers."

Tell her what you heard her say and ask if you are right.

Express comfort: "I am so sorry for how you have suffered."

Never look at your watch while she is talking.

FRED LOWERY
FROM "COVENANT MARRIAGE"

WHEN TIMES ARE TOUGH

ADMIT IT.

Acknowledge that there are differences between you, some of which might be important ones. Name them.

FACE IT.

Don't avoid conflict, particularly regarding areas of disagreement. A healthy relationship involves disagreeing in a respectful, loving manner.

CONFESS IT.

Be a big enough person to admit when you are wrong or do things that are unfair, immature, or spiteful. Don't be afraid of saying you're sorry.

VALUE IT.

God forbid that something should happen to one of you, but it might. Honor the privilege of marriage and all it means in your daily life.

LAUGH AT IT.

Keep your sense of humor! It makes forever a lot more bearable and fun.

KAY COLES JAMES
FROM "WHAT I WISH I'D KNOWN BEFORE I GOT MARRIED"

INAPPROPRIATE BEHAVIORS

1.
Calling your spouse inappropriate names

2.
Making assumptions

3.
Mind reading

4.
Laying on guilt

5.
Bringing up the past

6.
Attacking your spouse's family

7.
Making fun of or putting down your spouse

8.
Using "you" inappropriately (you always, you never)

9.
Assigning blame

10.
Rejecting or discrediting your spouse

FRED LOWERY
FROM "COVENANT MARRIAGE"

HOW DO YOU RATE?

- When you're on time but your spouse isn't, are you patient?
- When your spouse needs attention but you're focused on a task, are you understanding?
- When your spouse succeeds in his or her own sphere of strength, are you the enthusiastic cheerleader?
- Do you mention how much you've done in the past when you're trying to get the upper hand during a disagreement in the present?
- Do you ever use your spouse as the butt of your jokes or the target of your one-liners?
- Do you ever leave the impression with your mate that it's your way or the highway?
- When you're watching your favorite show or reading your favorite book but your mate wants to talk, are you willing to stop and listen?
- Do you keep short accounts or detailed records of hurts from the past?
- When your mate happens to be wrong, does your heart want to scream, "Gotcha! I knew I was right"?
- Are you willing to look for the best and overlook the worst?
- Are you willing to hang in there when the easier response would be to hang it up?

BOB RECCORD
FROM "BENEATH THE SURFACE"

WHAT MAKES
MARRIAGE WORTHWHILE?

12 QUOTES FROM COUPLES

- Our friendship and the ability to work together on common goals.
- Strong communication skills and building each other up constantly.
- We are each other's best friend and really enjoy being together.
- Spiritual commitment and commitment to each other.
- Companionship and sexual fulfillment.
- Mutual commitment and faith in God.
- We love each other and are best friends who inspire each other and stand together through the difficult times.
- We like each other, we let each other be ourselves, and we work together well.
- The support we give to each other during the good times and the not-so-good times.
- Laughter, and the fun we have together.
- Solid love and determination to make it work through the good and the bad.
- There is never a dull moment.

DAVID AND CLAUDIA ARP
CONDENSED FROM "THE SECOND HALF OF MARRIAGE"

5
Virtue

Strengthening your character

THE BEST THING TO GIVE...

to your enemy, forgiveness

&

to an opponent, tolerance

&

to a friend, your heart

&

to your child, a good example

&

to your mother, conduct that will make her proud of you

&

to yourself, respect

&

to all men, charity

FRANCIS MAITLAND BALFOUR
PHILOSOPHER

UNMANAGED ANGER

- Alienates those you love.

- Acts recklessly.

- Leads to foolish things.

- Causes mistakes.

- Creates quarrels.

- Loses control.

- Pays a heavy price.

- Ensnares you.

- Steals your peace.

- Speaks without thinking.

- Stirs up trouble.

- Produces strife.

SELECTED PROVERBS FROM "THE HOLY BIBLE"

PRIDE vs. HUMILITY

PRIDE PRODUCES MISUNDERSTANDINGS
Humility gives insight

PRIDE PROVOKES ARGUMENTS
Humility brings peace

PRIDE PREVENTS INTIMACY
Humility builds closeness

PRIDE POSTPONES RECONCILIATION
Humility admits mistakes

PRIDE PROMOTES ITSELF
Humility encourages others

MARK BELOKONNY
TEACHER AND PASTOR

SIX STEPS TO BREAK A BAD HABIT

1. **Is it really that bad?**
   You must be convinced it's harmful, stupid, or wrong.

2. **What are the consequences of not stopping?**
   Calculate the cost in time, money, and health.

3. **Does it grieve God, family, or friends?**
   Decide if you are willing to risk these relationships.

4. **Do you really want to change?**
   You will need both desire and perseverance.

5. **Can you admit your need for help?**
   If your answer is yes, you must take the next step.

6. **Will you seek support from others?**
   There is an array of help available for those who ask.

DR. JOSEPH C. ADRICH
PRESIDENT EMERITUS, MULTNOMAH BIBLE COLLEGE AND SEMINARY

TAKE COURAGE

COURAGE OF CONSCIENCE,
to do what is right.

COURAGE TO CONFORM,
to do what the law requires of you.

COURAGE TO COMMUNICATE,
to speak on issues of importance.

COURAGE TO CONSIDER,
to rethink preconceived notions.

COURAGE TO CARE,
to take personal responsibility and show love for others.

COURAGE TO CONFRONT,
to stand up to untruth and injustice.

COURAGE TO CHALLENGE,
to change the way you've always done it if it has been wrong.

COURAGE TO CORRECT,
to change your own behavior if it is wrong.

COURAGE TO CONFESS,
to acknowledge your personal wrongs toward others and God.

CHARLES CRISMIER
ADAPTED FROM "RENEWING THE SOUL OF AMERICA"

INTEGRITY IS...

§ taking responsibility for your words and actions.

§ keeping your promises to self and others.

§ being faithful in the little things.

§ telling the truth with love.

§ defending your ground in what is right.

§ maintaining virtue.

§ living a morally upright life.

§ making good and healthy choices.

§ standing firm in conflict.

§ never blaming or belittling others.

• admitting when you are wrong.

• doing what is moral and legal and ethical.

• holding to truth no matter what the consequences might be.

• maintaining an honorable reputation.

• respecting healthy boundaries.

• protecting self from temptation.

• avoiding the appearance of evil.

• showing respect for other people and their possessions.

• trusting yourself while doing what's right.

MARTV WILLIAMS
PASTOR OF FAMILV MINISTRIES

A MAN IS KNOWN BY...

The books he reads.

❧

The company he keeps.

❧

The praise he gives.

❧

The stories he tells.

❧

The notion of his eye.

〜

RALPH WALDO EMERSON
POET AND ESSAYIST

HOW TO ACHIEVE TRUE HUMILITY

1.

Admit your mistakes.

2.

Share credit with others.

3.

Refuse to honk your own horn.

4.

Be willing to give up your rights.

ROBERT JEFFRESS
ADAPTED FROM "THE SOLOMON SECRETS"

VIRTUE

DEVELOPING SELF-DISCIPLINE

1. START SMALL.
   Clean your room and then keep it clean. When something is out of place, train yourself to put it where it belongs. Then gradually extend that discipline to the rest of your home.

2. BE ON TIME.
   That may not sound very spiritual, but it's important. If you're supposed to be somewhere at a specific time, be there on time! Discipline your desires, activities, and demands so that you can arrive on time.

3. DO THE HARDEST JOB FIRST.
   That will prevent the most difficult tasks from being left undone.

4. ORGANIZE YOUR LIFE.
   Plan the use of your time rather than just reacting to circumstance. Use a calendar and make a daily list of the things you need to accomplish. If you don't control your time, everything else will.

5. ACCEPT CORRECTION.

Correction helps make you more disciplined, because it shows you what you need to avoid. Don't avoid criticism; accept it gladly.

6. PRACTICE SELF-DENIAL.

Learn to say no to your feelings. Occasionally deny yourself things that would be all right, just for the purpose of mastering yourself. Learn to do what you know to be right even if you don't feel like it.

7. WELCOME RESPONSIBILITY.

When you have an opportunity to do something that needs to be done, volunteer for it if you have a talent in that area. Welcoming responsibility forces you to organize yourself.

DR. JOHN MACARTHUR
PASTOR AND TEACHER

VIRTUE

FOUR KEYS TO VIRTUE

§

Love means to love that which is unlovable,
or it is no virtue at all.

§

Forgiving means to pardon the unpardonable,
or it is no virtue at all.

§

Faith means believing the unbelievable,
or it is no virtue at all.

§

Hope means hoping when things are hopeless,
or it is no virtue at all.

G. K. CHESTERTON
NOVELIST, POET, AND ESSAYIST, ADAPTED FROM "THE HERETICS"

THE TEST OF A GOOD PRINCIPLE

❧

It is true in almost every situation.

❧

It has stood the test of time.

❧

It is something that I would want my neighbor to practice.

❧

As found in the Bible, it is consistent with the plan of the Creator.

CHARLES CRISMIER
ADAPTED FROM "RENEWING THE SOUL OF AMERICA"

PROTECTING YOUR VALUES

PRINCIPLE #1:
Be Careful What You View

It has been said that the eyes are the window to the soul. That being the case, it's critically important to monitor what goes in the eye because of its impact on the soul.

PRINCIPLE #2:
Be Careful What You Think

It has been said that we can't always help what comes into our minds, but we have all the control in the world over what stays there.

PRINCIPLE #3:
Be Careful What You Feel

In our day, it seems that emotion too often sits in the driver's seat of our lives. But emotions are significantly unpredictable.

PRINCIPLE #4:
Be Careful Where You Go

Our feet can take us in good directions and lousy directions.

BOB RECCORD
CONDENSED FROM "BENEATH THE SURFACE"

SEVEN GIFTS

God grant us...

1. THE GIFT OF UNDERSTANDING—
   by which Your precepts may enlighten our minds.

2. THE GIFT OF COUNSEL—
   by which we may follow Your footsteps on the paths of righteousness.

3. THE GIFT OF COURAGE—
   by which we may ward off the enemy's attacks.

4. THE GIFT OF KNOWLEDGE—
   by which we can distinguish good from evil.

5. THE GIFT OF PIETY—
   by which we may acquire compassionate hearts.

6. THE GIFT OF FEAR—
   by which we may draw back from evil and submit to what is good.

7. THE GIFT OF WISDOM—
   by which we may taste fully the life-giving sweetness of Your love.

ADAPTED FROM BONAVENTURA
13TH-CENTURY MONK

LET ME BE...

obedient without arguing,

pure without corruption,

merry without lightness,

sober without dullness,

true without doubleness,

fearing Thee without desperation,

trusting in Thee without presumption.

JOHN COSIN
ADAPTED FROM "THE BOOK OF PRAYER"

CULTIVATE THESE QUALITIES

- Unity of heart and singleness of purpose.

- Joy in God's creation.

- Contentment and trust.

- Freedom from covetousness.

- Modesty and temperance in all things.

- Receiving material provision gratefully.

- Using money without abusing money.

- Availability.

- Giving joyfully and generously.

RICHARD J. FOSTER
FROM "THE CHALLENGE OF THE DISCIPLINED LIFE"

EIGHT VALUABLE DISCIPLINES

1.

THE DISCIPLINE OF SELFLESSNESS

There is a clarity to our vision when we completely forget ourselves and concentrate solely on the task before us.

2.

THE DISCIPLINE OF WAITING

Few things produce character like learning how to wait.

3.

THE DISCIPLINE OF SUFFERING

Suffering and difficulty is something that can nourish us even as it causes pain.

4.

THE DISCIPLINE OF SOCIAL MERCY

Authentic faith is marked by a compassionate response toward those the world tends to forget, whether these persons are poor, imprisoned, disabled, sick, or mentally challenged.

5.

THE DISCIPLINE OF FORGIVENESS
Forgiveness offers tremendous personal blessing.

6.

THE DISCIPLINE OF MOURNING
Mourning invites us to a deeper, more reflective life.

7.

THE DISCIPLINE OF CONTENTMENT
Without contentment we will always be restless.

8.

THE DISCIPLINE OF SACRIFICE
Once we adopt a heart of sacrifice, everything else tends to fall into place.

GARY L THOMAS
ADAPTED FROM "AUTHENTIC FAITH"

CHARACTER IS DEVELOPED BY...

Thought

Choice

Courage

Determination

JOHN HILL LUTHER
FIRST PRESIDENT OF BAYLOR FEMALE COLLEGE

6
Health

Nurturing a long and satisfying life

REGULAR EXERCISE

Being physically active for at least 30 minutes a day, three or more days a week, has these benefits:

§ helps build and maintain healthy bones, muscles, and joints.

§ builds endurance and muscular strength.

§ helps manage weight.

§ lowers risk factors for heart disease, colon cancer, and type 2 diabetes.

§ helps control blood pressure.

§ promotes psychological well-being and self-esteem.

§ reduces feelings of depression and anxiety.

§ helps to reduce your risk of developing or dying from heart disease.

U.S. DEPARTMENT OF HEALTH AND HUMAN SERVICES

HEALTH

TAKING YOUR MEDICINE

1. **Take control of your own health.**

   Consider yourself the boss; your doctor, pharmacist, and nurse *work for you*.

2. **Educate yourself.**

   Don't be afraid to ask questions of your doctor and pharmacist. If you have questions, write them down and bring them with you next time you see them. Go on the Internet and look up your medication—learn all you can about the medication.

3. **Explore your options.**

   There is almost always a less expensive line of medication that is just as effective.

4. **Don't follow old wives' tales.**

   When it comes to dosage instructions, listen to your doctor or pharmacist, not grandma.

5. **If you forget to take your medicine...**

   ...at the time prescribed, generally, it is better to miss a dosage than to double up. It would be best to keep a medication diary.

JOHN COOPER
PHARMACIST

BEFORE YOU TAKE
ANY KIND OF MEDICINE...

MAKE SURE YOU KNOW:

- What it is.

- Why you should take it.

- If it could make you feel sleepy or cause some other problem for you.

- When to take it.

- How much to take.

- How long to take it.

- What you should *not* have while taking your medicine.

U.S. FOOD AND DRUG ADMINISTRATION

TEN SIGNS OF BURNOUT

1.
LACK OF ENERGY

2.
LOSS OF ENJOYMENT

3.
APATHY

4.
AVOIDING PEOPLE

5.
HARD TO GET MOTIVATED

6.
LOWERED PRODUCTIVITY

7.
TROUBLE WITH SLEEP

8.
CHANGE IN APPETITE

9.
POOR CONCENTRATION

10.
DIFFICULTY MAKING DECISIONS

DR. STEVE STEPHENS
PSYCHOLOGIST AND SEMINAR SPEAKER

HOW TO FIND RELIEF FROM BURNOUT

Take a vacation.
Even one day off can renew your outlook. Your body requires rest. It requires even more when you're stressed. Take it easy when you need to.

Take up a sport.
Lack of exercise and poor diet are big time-robbers and can contribute to depression. Burnout and poor health together are depression double-whammies. Avoid that extra risk and treat yourself to extra energy.

Take time for friends.
Socializing gives perspective. There's comfort in knowing you're not alone. It also provides brainstorming opportunities. You can pool ideas with people who are experiencing the same dilemmas.

Take a break with a good book.
Treat yourself to some time in that novel you've been wanting to read. Feed your brain and your spirit.

Take control.
There's hardly anything worse than feeling overwhelmed and out of control. Learn to shrug more away. Take charge of those areas where you can make a difference—even if it's a very small difference.

RHONDA RHEA
COLUMNIST AND SEMINAR SPEAKER

TEN WAYS TO RELIEVE THE PRESSURE

1.

Enroll in a karate, kickboxing, or aerobics class.

2.

Practice the law of opposites. On days when you interact with a lot of people, get away from everyone by taking a walk, sitting at a park, or going to lunch by yourself. On days spent alone, get out with other people by meeting someone for coffee.

3.

Buy a joke book and keep it in your desk. Take a five-minute break, read a few jokes, and have a laugh.

4.

Stop working for 10 or 15 minutes, dim the lights, light a candle or two, and breathe deeply. Pray and ask God to help you through this stressful time.

5.

Learn to say no. For most people, stress comes from being over-committed.

6.

Ask yourself, "Will what I'm worried about make a difference in a month or a year?" If not, let it go.

7.

Create a stress box. Write down anything causing stress and put it in the box. That simple act of surrender just might help you feel better.

8.

Chop some wood for your fireplace, rake up some leaves, shovel the sidewalk, or mow the lawn (depending on the season, of course). You'll get the benefit of doing something physical and getting another chore done.

9.

Close your office door, get down on the carpet, and do some gentle stretching exercises for a few minutes. If it helps, pop in a favorite mellow CD.

10.

Go for a drive in the countryside, listen to some piano or acoustical guitar music, or just ride in silence.

CONDENSED FROM "REV" MAGAZINE

HOW TO AVOID GETTING SICK

Wash your hands often. You can pick up cold germs easily, even when shaking someone's hand or touching doorknobs or handrails.

§

Avoid people with colds when possible.

§

If you sneeze or cough, do it into a tissue and then throw the tissue away.

§

Clean surfaces you touch with a germ-killing disinfectant.

§

Don't touch your nose, eyes, or mouth. Germs can enter your body easily by these paths.

U.S. FOOD AND DRUG ADMINISTRATION

ADVANTAGES OF WALKING

1.

Helps rid your body of harmful stress chemicals.

2.

Increases your metabolism and helps prevent excess weight gain.

3.

Tones your muscles and strengthens your bones.

4.

Improves your energy.

5.

Reduces your risk of heart disease.

6.

Calms the brain, decreasing anxiety and elevating mood.

7.

Provides a convenient, nonpainful, nonstressful
way of becoming physically fit.

8.

Fits into your life just about anytime, anywhere.

9.

There's nothing to it, but to do it.

KATHRINE BUTLER
CONDENSED FROM "STRESSBUSTERS"

NINE WAYS
TO SPICE UP YOUR WORKOUT

1. **Pick several activities you like.**
    Vary walking sessions with line dancing, softball, or tennis.
    If you enjoy water aerobics, try a tai chi or aquatic class. If
    you love ballroom dancing, sign up for some tango lessons.

2. **Keep a record.**
    Note what you did and for how long. "It's a great motiva-
    tional technique," says Wayne Westcott, Ph.D., fitness
    research director of the South Shore YMCA in Quincy,
    Massachusetts.

3. **If the weather outside is frightful, find an indoor alternative.**
    Swim or exercise in an indoor pool, or work out with a
    home video. Sign up for a three-month class in resistance
    training or low-impact aerobics.

4. **Make exercise convenient.**
    Look for a facility close to home or work. If you can't find
    anything nearby, use your lunch hour to take a brisk walk.

5. **Plan an active vacation, then train for it.**
    Getting in shape for a walking tour, kayaking adventure, or
    cycling trip will give extra purpose to your regular work-
    out.

6. ***Try a personal trainer.***

   If you want to start a weight-lifting program but the equipment looks more like a torture chamber than a way to shape up, consider a few sessions with a personal trainer to get you started safely.

7. ***Treat yourself to new gear.***

   A bright warm-up suit, new running shoes, rubber resistance bands, or a giant ball can put some welcome pizzazz into your regular routine.

8. ***Combine activities.***

   Tape your favorite late-night TV program to watch while you're pedaling a stationary bike. Do some bicep curls with hand weights when you've been put on hold on the telephone.

9. ***Get a dog, or borrow one from a neighbor.***

   There's nothing like canine companionship for exploring new neighborhoods or paths.

ELIZABETH POPE
FROM "NEW CHOICES" MAGAZINE

LIVING THE GOOD LIFE

Record your progress toward healthy living in a small notebook.
This is your daily wellness journal, where you'll keep track of things like how much water you consume, fruit you eat, and exercise you've done.

Think of the person you want to be in 10, 30, or 50 years.
Picture the energy, physical ability, and productivity you want. Think of the gift you'd give yourself and others by taking care of yourself today.

Know the facts about how small efforts add up to your benefit.
There's substantial evidence that even thirty minutes of moderate activity accumulated over the course of one day, every day, can significantly reduce the risk of heart disease, strokes, and some cancers.

Give yourself permission to start over with your exercise, food plan, and spiritual growth as often as you'd like.
Nothing is more defeating than an all-or-nothing attitude. Remind yourself: "I may renegotiate my goals—any and all good intentions—as often as necessary. I can start over as many times as I need to or want."

Give some thought to making exercise enjoyable.
It's essential to have some measure of joyful anticipation for whatever activity you choose, otherwise it simply won't become a consistent part of your life.

Think of ways to celebrate your meals.

Place a single flower in a bud vase on the table or light a candle to create a peaceful atmosphere. Surround yourself with beauty and grace, especially at mealtimes.

Don't let your exercise routine become one of those things that keeps you too busy to do things with people you love.

Yes, exercise is important to health, but never more important than the other components of wellness, and when it's out of balance it's downright unhealthy.

Be aware of how much time you have alone to be still.

Emotional healing generally cannot happen in the midst of chaotic, busy schedules, and staying overly busy is one of the ways many people use to avoid dealing with their issues.

Learn to ask for what you need.

There's nothing wrong with asking for a favor or some assistance from someone you trust. Be willing to make yourself vulnerable; you'll discover that life doesn't have to be so solitary and hard.

Think about the choices you can make to change things you control.

What actions could you take to make your life a better one? What could you do daily to live a healthier and more fulfilling life?

RUTH MCGINNIS
CONDENSED FROM "LIVING THE GOOD LIFE"

HEALTH

EATING WELL

Take time to eat, seated at a table or at least in a chair,
undistracted by the television and the hustle and bustle of life.

§

Give thanks before you start.

§

Put your fork down and chew each bite thoroughly and
swallow before picking up the utensil again.

§

Notice periodically if you feel full so you don't eat
more than your body needs.

§

Remember to take time to savor the ritual as much as the food
and to breathe deeply while you eat.

§

Refuse to eat while driving the car or on the run.

RUTH MCGINNIS
CONDENSED FROM "LIVING THE GOOD LIFE"

HELP YOUR CHILDREN
BUILD STRONG BONES BY:

1.

Stressing the importance of eating at least three servings
of low-fat or nonfat dairy products per day.

2.

Staying away from fast food, which is generally low in calcium.

3.

Encouraging our kids to drink fewer soft drinks.

4.

Having our kids exercise regularly.

5.

Including calcium supplements in their diet.

GENETTA ADAIR
FROM "FOCUS ON THE FAMILY" MAGAZINE

STRESS BREAKS AT WORK

1. Read the comics or your favorite columnist in the papers.

2. Read a poem.

3. Hear a favorite song with a tape recorder and headphones.

4. Relax with a cup of herbal tea.

5. Close your eyes and visualize yourself skiing down a slope.

6. Exchange a quick neck or back rub with a colleague.

7. Plan something fun for that evening or weekend.

8. Lay your head on the desk for a five-minute nap.

9. Walk to the café next door for a cold drink.

10. Check the movie schedule in the daily paper.

11. Call a friend and plan a lunch date.

12. Make a list of what you want for Christmas or your birthday.

13. Praise a secretary or coworker for a job well done.

14. Browse through a catalog or art book.

15. Look at travel books and brochures and plan your next vacation.

16. Play with a toy you keep at the office, such as a yo-yo, kaleidoscope, paddle ball, or dart board.

17. Take a walk around the block or around the office.

18. Work on a crossword puzzle.

19. Tell someone a joke.

20. Breathe deeply or meditate for five minutes.

21. Wash your face.

22. Play the perfect hole of golf in your imagination. Choose your favorite golf course.

ANN MCGEE-COOPER
FROM "YOU DON'T HAVE TO GO HOME FROM WORK EXHAUSTED"

THE BALANCING ACT

Simplify.

Need help with housecleaning? Consider hiring a cleaning person once a week. Feel like you don't have time? Say no to things you don't want to do or don't have time to do.

Be grateful.

Even in the midst of the most hectic and stressful times of life, there are things for which we can be thankful. Reflecting on the good things in our lives helps keep an all-important balance in our outlook.

Be a kid and play.

Get down in the dirt and help the kids make mud pies, watch a movie with them, or have a long chat over coffee with your teen. Give your family one-on-one time.

Pay attention to yourself.

If you don't stay healthy, you'll be less able to handle the stress of work and home.

Stop procrastinating.

It takes more energy fretting over not doing a project than actually doing it. So save your energy for better things and just get started.

RAGAN COMMUNICATIONS

HOW TO CHILL OUT

- Spend an afternoon at the biggest bookstore you can find. Slide into an overstuffed chair, sip coffee, read some fiction, take a nap, pray for a while.

- Schedule a weekly game of tennis or racquetball or a round of golf for a regular chill-out time.

- Take up gardening. While some people don't have the patience for the process of gardening, you might just find how relaxing it can be to dig in the soil and grow wonderful flowers or foods.

- Find a chill-out spot within an hour's drive from home. You might discover a favorite coffee hangout, a lake, or a state park. Each time you arrive at your destination, have it be your special place to just sit and read.

- Develop a hobby. Choose from hundreds, such as antiquing, genealogy research, model trains, collecting, amateur radios, and more. Do an on-line search for hobbies.

- Take a martial arts class that focuses more on stretching or exercise, rather than on fancy fighting moves.

- Go bowling. For some reason, there's something both nostalgic and therapeutic about renting bowling shoes and picking up a solid ball and hurling it at ten pins.

FROM "REV" MAGAZINE

HEALTH

LETTING GO OF WORRIES

1. REVIEW THE FACTS.

Focus your attention on what is, not on what if. A mind that feeds on the facts is less likely to fall prey to a frenzied imagination that casts illusions as reality.

2. REQUIRE A PLAN.

Developing a plan can hold anxiety at bay. Just knowing that you're taking concrete steps to work on a problem can bring relief.

3. RECONNECT WITH THE PRESENT.

Many of our worries come from a tendency to overestimate the probability of a harmful event and to exaggerate its potential negative effect.

4. REACH OUT TO PEOPLE.

When your worries seem overwhelming, resist the temptation to isolate yourself, withdraw, and shrink back in the shadows.

5. RESPECT YOUR NEED FOR RENEWAL.

Your body will never lie to you. If you feel restless or on edge and worries are keeping you up at night, pay attention to your physical needs. Consider consistent exercise and good sleep.

6. REDUCE STIMULATION.

Even small adjustments that reduce stimulation can have a positive emotional impact and diminish your worries. Quiet some of the outside noise for a week or two, and see if your world seems like a more enjoyable place to live.

7. ROCK WITH LAUGHTER.

Laughter can promote sound mental and physical health, deflect anxious thoughts, and help us cope more effectively with overwhelming pressures.

8. REFUSE TO ASSUME THE WORST.

A concern is a concern, not a major disaster. A temporary setback is just that, not a permanent failure cast in stone for all eternity. Keep that in mind the next time you start to assume the worst.

9. RELY ON FAITH.

Let's allow our anxieties to be a reminder to surrender ourselves fully to God in trust and humility. Let's use worry to trigger a prayer.

PAM VREDEVELT
ADAPTED FROM "LETTING GO OF WORRY AND ANXIETY"

ANXIETY CURE

1. *Take control of your fear.*
   The difference between panic and recovery is that recovered sufferers have overcome their fear of panic.

2. *Drop the "what-ifs" in your life.*
   Change your attitude to "So what?"

3. *Overcome your personal passivity.*
   Anxiety doesn't take your control away; you surrender it.

4. *Increase your power by finding out all you can about your anxiety and fear.*
   Knowledge and understanding are your allies.

5. *Be compassionate toward yourself.*
   Too many sufferers are their own worst enemies. Don't self-accuse ("I'm stupid," etc.).

6. *Don't let your problem dominate your life.*
   Relegate it to a secondary position and give priority to living.

7. *Find a good support group.*
   A group of understanding peers can help build your personal power.

8. *Beware of the pitfalls of self-pity.*
   Ask yourself, "What can I do about it?" instead of saying, "Woe is me!"

9. *Never, never, never, never give up.*

ARCHIBALD HART
FROM "THE ANXIETY CURE: YOU CAN FIND EMOTIONAL TRANQUILITY AND WHOLENESS"

HEALTHY SELF-ACCEPTANCE

1.
Have patience with all things but first with yourself.

2.
Never confuse your mistakes with your value as a human being.

3.
*Remember that you're a perfectly valuable, creative,
worthwhile person simply because you exist.*

4.
*Never forget that healthy self-acceptance is
the core of a peaceful mind.*

ADAPTED FROM ST. FRANCIS DE SALES
17TH-CENTURY SPIRITUAL ADVISOR

7
The Second Half

Improving with time

FIVE TIPS FOR STAYING YOUNG

1.

Your mind is not old, keep developing it.

2.

Your humor is not over, keep enjoying it.

3.

Your strength is not gone, keep using it.

4.

Your opportunities have not vanished, keep pursuing them.

5.

God is not dead, keep seeking Him.

CHARLES R. SWINDOLL
FROM "THE TALE OF THE TARDY OXCART"

ROMANCE AFTER THE KIDS
LEAVE HOME

Be affectionate.
We all like to be nurtured and cherished. A phone call, love note, bouquet of flowers, kiss, or wink across the room can add romance to your relationship.

Be adventurous.
Try a little spontaneity. If you always make love in the evening, try mornings. Also try some variety where you make love.

Be in shape.
Fitness walking several times a week gives you energy and helps you stay in shape. Face it, when you feel good about your body, you feel better about romance!

Be playful.
When time is limited, we remind ourselves that whatever we do to promote romance is half the fun.

Be in love for a lifetime.
Look forward to growing old together and loving each other along the way. Romance doesn't have to die. It can grow through all the years if you continue to show your love in physical ways plus loving words and deeds.

DAVID AND CLAUDIA ARP
FROM "LIFEWISE" MAGAZINE

ADJUSTING TO
YOUR SPOUSE'S RETIREMENT

❦ Make decisions together and divide chores so you each have your area of expertise.

❦ Most problems can be solved easily if approached with a light, humorous tone rather than a heavy, demanding attitude.

❦ Don't feel guilty if some days you just can't take it any longer and want to get away. It's beneficial for each of you to spend time alone or with friends. You come back to your marriage refreshed and often with a new topic of conversation to share.

❦ Be honest about your needs. Your husband wants to please you, but he is not a mind reader. If he is doing something that bugs you, tell him. You may be misinterpreting his actions.

❦ Retirement for men ranks high on the list of major sources of stress, so have some consideration for what your husband is going through. Many men equate self-esteem with their jobs and feel worthless out of the workplace. Remind him that he is loved for who he is, not what he does.

❦ Learn to count your blessings instead of compiling your complaints!

MARY ANN COOK
ADAPTED FROM "LIFEWISE" MAGAZINE, AS PRINTED IN "BETTER LIFE!"

ENJOY YOUR RETIREMENT

Keep Physically Fit
Develop a regular physical exercise regimen.
Walk thirty minutes to an hour with your spouse or a friend.
Take up a sport that makes you sweat!
Find and keep good doctors.
Get a physical every year and do what the doctors tell you to do.

Keep Mentally Fit
Keep a personal journal.
Work crossword puzzles.
Have a continuous jigsaw puzzle going with the grandkids.
Get a computer—e-mail relatives and friends.
Take a class for something you always wanted to learn.

Get to Know Your Kids Better
Talk about your concerns, future dreams, and goals.
Show an interest in their hobbies.
Let them know that you pray for them.
Help with their projects like painting the house or finishing the basement.
Encourage rather than give advice during tough times.

Spend Time with Your Grandkids
Call often or correspond by e-mail.
Show an interest in their sports, hobbies, and friends.
Remember special days with cards and small gifts.
Take them camping or fishing.
Ask about the most important ways you can pray for them.

Develop a Cross-Section of Friends
Don't spend all your time with "old retired" people!
Organize a block party or neighborhood potluck.
Help neighbors with large projects.
Join the men's or women's group at church.
Adopt a single parent and their children.

Bless Your Community
Join Habitat for Humanity.
Be a mentor at the Boys and Girls Club.
Volunteer as a reader at an elementary school.
Teach a Sunday school class.
Organize a team to pick up litter.

Treat Yourself Well
Pursue a sport, hobby, or cultural interest.
Spend time at the bookstore or library.
Attend high school sport events and cheer hard for the home team.
Occasionally eat out at a swanky restaurant and go to a show or concert.
Take your vitamins.

RICH SCHMIDT, PH.D.
RETIRED FROM OREGON STATE DEPARTMENT OF EDUCATION

REVITALIZE YOUR
RETIREMENT ROUTINES

§ Get up early.

§ Give yourself assignments and deadlines for important jobs.

§ Make reading and writing key endeavors in your routine.

§ Be eager to learn new things on subjects of interest.

§ Schedule a time when you exercise and see your friends.

§ Use math skills to keep up with your various financial needs.

§ Go with others on a field trip or plan to see faraway places.

§ Pick a special friend to sit with at lunch—and share a surprise treat.

§ Enjoy active physical exercise four days a week.

§ At close of day thank God for specific blessings and your vibrant life!

CHARLOTTE ADELSPERGER
INSPIRATIONAL AUTHOR AND SPEAKER

20 REASONS GRANDPARENTS
ARE IMPORTANT

1. We have more time.
2. We have experience.
3. We can teach skills.
4. We have gathered wisdom.
5. We can tell great stories.
6. We remember the way things used to be.
7. We don't have anything to prove.
8. We can be there to support.
9. We are great childcare providers.
10. We know the value of education.
11. We are good listeners.
12. We can encourage both our children and our grandchildren.
13. We know the importance of character.
14. We hold family history and traditions.
15. We realize that "being" is more important than "doing."
16. We provide security and stability.
17. We have learned what is temporary and what really lasts.
18. We love both our children and our grandchildren.
19. We have perspective.
20. We have a faith to share.

COLLECTED FROM VARIOUS GRANDPARENTS

TEN WAYS TO TOUCH
GRANDKIDS FROM AFAR

1. **E-mail is in,** but just asking "How are you?" will usually get you a one-word answer: "Fine." Ask specific questions like "Who is your coach?" "Tell me about your new friend," or "What were you doing last Sunday afternoon when I was thinking about you?"

2. **The family letter** will never mean as much to a child as the letter that is meant for him personally. Mail is like a hug from grandparents.

3. **Make correspondence educational.** Kids love to learn. Write about the birds and animals, stars, storms, and cloud formations you've seen. Write about family history.

4. **Include grandchildren in your travels** by sending them videos, cassette recordings, and photos of the places you go. Tell about the smells, colors, and tastes. Ask the tour guide to say hello to them by name.

5. **In times of failure,** grandkids need positive affirmation, even if it's only by telephone: "I love you whether you win or not," "Hang in there," and "There's always next time."

6. **Interest and concern** needs to be shown for their everyday lives, not just special days like birthdays or graduation. Telephone and talk to each child for no particular reason.

7. **Send gifts when appropriate,** but sometimes send surprises like a small check attached to a note suggesting that the receiver take the whole family out for ice cream cones.

8. **Keep your word.** If you said you would send or do something, don't forget. Those disappointments may never be forgotten, nor forgiven.

9. **Carry photos of your grandchildren in your purse or wallet.** Ask for updates because you know they are getting more beautiful all the time.

10. **Never stop praying for them and saying "I love you,"** even when they are grown.

BARBARA BAUMGARDNER, COLUMNIST
CONDENSED FROM "THE TIE THAT BINDS", AS PUBLISHED IN "RV COMPANION" MAGAZINE

DO'S AND DON'TS
OF GRANDPARENTING

DO believe that kids need their grandparents.
   DON'T forget what it was like when you were their age.

DO be willing to discover their passions, dreams, and interests.
   DON'T give up if the relationship gets difficult.

DO praise loudly, criticize gently.
   DON'T let differences in behavior or appearance keep you from
   getting close.

DO be patient as you teach them life skills.
   DON'T be negative, grumpy, or irritable.

DO take time and give time.
   DON'T think that they don't care about your opinion.

DO share values and virtues that are eternally important.
   DON'T undermine or put down their parents.

DO let kids be kids.
   DON'T underestimate the impact a caring grandparent can have.

BECKY STEPHENS
GRANDMOTHER OF 18

HOW GRANDPARENTS CAN ENCOURAGE GRANDCHILDREN

1. *Introduce* your grandchild to new ideas about the world around her.

2. *Talk about* your own response to things, your own ideas. Let them know who you are. Share your enthusiasms. Help them get turned on to life through a diversity of experiences and ideas.

3. *Teach them* your skills and hobbies.

4. *Support new* experiences and special projects.

5. *They love* to help and have jobs to do but will require your guidance. Some possibilities are juicing oranges, polishing silver, doing yard work, washing the car, helping with younger children. You will be able to think of other activities. Such projects make them feel good and promote a sense of responsibility.

6. *Take them* seriously, listen carefully, and take time.

7. *Never forget* to bring along your sense of humor.

DR. LILLIAN CARSON
FROM "THE ESSENTIAL GRANDPARENT"

SUCCESSFUL VOLUNTEERING

❧

Do be flexible.
It is rare to find the "perfect" fit right away. Keep an open mind—
you might discover something new that interests you.

❧

Do be persistent.
Volunteer coordinators are often busy, so don't assume
they're not interested in you if they don't call you right away.

❧

Do attend orientation meetings.
Keep in mind that informed volunteers are the best volunteers.
These meetings will help you do the best job possible.

❧

Do take necessary training classes.
Ask about them before you decide to get involved and
be prepared to learn what will be needed.

Do be responsible.
Show up on time and follow through with your commitments.
People will be depending on you.

Don't expect to start at the top.
You have to work hard and prove your worth before
you are given more responsibility.

Don't think that volunteering has to be a group effort.
You can start your own volunteer program and
do it on your own time.

***Do expect to get plenty of personal enjoyment and satisfaction
from your volunteer experiences.***

THE PRUDENTIAL SPIRIT OF COMMUNITY INITIATIVE
FROM "CATCH THE SPIRIT!"

KEEP LIFE UPBEAT

1. *Be an inverted paranoid*—believe that the whole world is conspiring to do only good things to me.

2. *Be a quick forgiver*—I know I have been forgiven for much, therefore I want to forgive much. Besides, I don't have time to waste in unforgiveness.

3. *Be optimistic*—believing the best in people and circumstances is a sure way to find the best. Pessimists usually find what they are looking for!

4. *Be thankful*—always giving thanks keeps my eyes on God as my provider and a smile on my face. Thankful people are also much more fun to be around.

5. *Be an encourager*—encouragers make me feel better, stronger, and more capable of accomplishing my dreams. I want to do the same with every person I meet.

6. *Be spontaneous*—take advantage of situations and circumstances. I've met people in every conceivable place who ended up dramatically impacting my life, or vice versa. I have a sense of urgency and a do-it-now attitude.

7. *Be a giver*—I tell people, "If I can be of any service to you or your children, anytime, anywhere, anyplace, just call." It gives me a chance to be a giver, and that's my greatest joy! The only problem is that they don't call often enough.

8. *Be positive*—not enough can ever be said about the benefits of having a positive attitude. Being positive has the potential of turning the worst situations into victories.

9. *Smile a lot and laugh at life*—adversity is a stepping stone, and mistakes are opportunities to learn, not signs of failure. Why not laugh in the midst of challenges that are good for you?

10. *Live life with enthusiasm*—I live only once, so why not give it my all? I believe I can do far more than I think I can, and enthusiasm helps me try harder.

11. *Enjoy life*—I enjoy life. For many years I have collected 1936 Fords, chased down our family genealogy, and worked to establish our company library of personal development books. It has brought enjoyment to me and to many other people as well.

12. *Find a hobby you enjoy*—hiking, scuba diving, tennis, golf, swimming, biking, and fishing are a few of my hobbies. Then no matter where I am, I have something I enjoy doing.

13. *Look for people to help*—I get up every morning excited about the person I might help that day. The actual help will take many different forms, but when I'm actively looking for someone, I seldom miss.

PAUL J. MEYER
FROM "UNLOCKING YOUR LEGACY"

THE SECOND HALF

CULTIVATE AN ACTIVE MIND

Spend time with curious people, especially children.

Keep a journal to record questions and insights.

Look up unfamiliar words you find while reading.

Learn a new language.

Cultivate the art of asking for feedback.

Become a student of human nature.

Pursue eclectic interests.

Take time to contemplate.

ED ROWELL
CONDENSED FROM "GO THE DISTANCE"

THINGS I WISH I'D DONE SOONER

*Not worried about the future when the present
was real and alive before me.*

*Paid more attention when my parents and
grandparents told about their past.*

Hugged our children more.

*Told my dad and other veterans how much I appreciate
what they did for our country.*

Taken more luxurious baths and read more captivating books.

Forgotten more grudges and given more forgiveness.

*Used my antique teacups instead of
just looking at them in the china hutch.*

Gone to more operas, ballets, and concerts.

Worked less and played more.

Spent more time building friendships.

BARBARA DARLAND
RETIRED PROFESSOR, WRITER, ARTIST

LEAVING A LEGACY

HOW I WANT TO BE REMEMBERED...

HE LOVED GOD FIRST.

Without God, I am nothing and have nothing of value to pass on through my legacy. I love Him because He loves me more than I can imagine and because of all He has done for me.

HE LOVED HIS FAMILY AND EXTENDED FAMILY.

You can't ask for anything more precious than family. They are there with you when things are going well and when things are going bad. I love my family!

HE WAS A GIVER.

Meeting needs is my opportunity to give back, to help, to serve, to bless—and besides, it's a whole lot of fun!

HE WAS AN ENCOURAGER.

I want people to walk away from me feeling more encouraged and more excited about life than before they saw me.

HE FORGAVE!

There is nothing in the world so important that I can't forgive another person. The freedom and liberty that forgiveness brings is indescribable, and I do all I can to liberate others as well.

HE KEPT HIS WORD.

I believe that keeping my word is of utmost importance. I have made promises many years ago that are written in my will—when I die, my promises will still be kept.

HE HONORED GOD WITH HIS LIFE.

My hope is that everything I do in life will be a testament of God's goodness. God deserves to be honored with everything I am and ever will be.

HE ALWAYS HAD A POSITIVE ATTITUDE.

This includes never giving up; serving; loving; giving; seeing the best in others; and much, much more.

HE WAS A ROLE MODEL.

My objective is to prepare my children and grandchildren for the best future imaginable   in every sense of the word.

HE CONSISTENTLY HELPED OTHERS.

A handout is one thing, but a hand up is so much better. A gift or act of service once a year is nice, but change usually comes through long-term help—I believe that it is the least I can do.

PAUL J. MEYER
CONDENSED FROM "UNLOCKING YOUR LEGACY"

THINGS SPOUSES NEED TO DO
WHILE BOTH ARE HEALTHY

Wills and Trusts

- Prepare a will or trust and update it every year.
- Have a directive to family physicians and power of attorney for health care.
- Make a list of important possessions and who will inherit them.
- Name an executor.
- Put these important documents in a bank safety deposit box.
- Have keys made for each spouse, the executor, and one other responsible adult.

Familiar Contacts

- In a conspicuous place, post a list of contact information for children, close friends, doctor, pharmacy, and emergency services.
- Give a copy of the list to a close friend and one adult child.
- When traveling, give a copy of your itinerary to family and trusted neighbors.

Finances

- Keep a list of all active credit card account and phone numbers.
- Carry an extra copy of this information with you when you travel.
- Place a record of bank accounts, pin numbers, and access codes for investment funds and insurance in a home safe or deposit box.
- Post a list of regularly scheduled bills with amounts and due dates.

Learn how to…

- Shut off power and/or reset breaker switch.
- Turn off water to house.
- Change a tire.
- Check oil and other car fluids.
- Start the lawnmower.
- Set timer for irrigation system.
- Use six common tools.
- Change the propane on the barbecue.

RICH SCHMIDT, PH.D.
RETIRED OREGON STATE DEPARTMENT OF EDUCATION

AGING

Don't **resist**—welcome it.

Don't **ignore**—accept it.

Don't **dread**—embrace it.

Don't **panic**—plan for it.

Don't **regret**—appreciate it.

Don't **complain**—enjoy it.

TRESS VAN DIEST
AGE 93!

A FINAL PRAYER

Give me grace, good Lord...

to count the world as nothing,

to set my mind firmly on You,

to be content to be alone,

to depend on Your comfort,

to suffer adversity patiently,

to be joyful for troubles,

to walk the narrow way that leads to life,

to keep the final hour in mind.

THOMAS MORE
16TH-CENTURY POLITICIAN

8
Tough Times

Getting through the struggles

GOD'S MERCY

When tears are the only language you know, God hears.

When darkness envelops your way, God sees.

When pain forces you off course, God stabilizes.

When loss wears you down, God comforts.

When grief suspends your progress and saps hope, God remains.

KARI WEST
FROM "DARE TO TRUST, DARE TO HOPE AGAIN"

WHAT SURVIVORS SAY

1. I will examine the future and let it guide what I do in the present.

2. No matter what happens, I will not allow myself to be defeated. I will keep on trying and will not give up.

3. I am a fortunate person, regardless of what I have experienced.

4. I will take advantage of every available opportunity.

5. I can accept my imperfections and learn to enjoy life and give to others.

6. I can find meaning in situations and events that involve suffering or great loss.

7. I will not allow myself to behave as a victim.

8. I'm determined to keep pushing ahead.

9. I am willing to grow, change, and learn new roles.

10. I want to be involved with people who will build me up and help me grow.

11. I can face the challenges of life and handle the stresses and crises of life without denying their existence or giving up.

H. NORMAN WRIGHT
CONDENSED FROM "WILL MY LIFE EVER BE THE SAME?"

EMOTIONAL HEALING TAKES TIME

§ **Time gives you rest.** We all need "downtime." In fact, when you push yourself too hard for too long, your body will eventually break down in some way.

§ **Time enlarges your focus.** Because of your wounds, your mind naturally constricts to focus on your own needs, your own feelings, and your own recovery. Over time, your focus will grow to include those around you. You'll gain a more balanced perspective about your own needs and those of others.

§ **Time helps you get all the facts.** Time helps you gain a truer understanding of yourself and your situation. Over time, you can get past the pain and start seeing the real issues.

§ **Time lets you see how things turn out.** In the wake of a traumatic loss, we all tend to think the future looks bleak. But over time, the future unfolds more brightly than we expect.

§ **Time allows you to balance out your life.** After a loss, people sometimes realize their own imbalances. Maybe they've been too selfish, too serious, too frivolous, too lazy, too talkative, or too quiet.

THOMAS A. WHITEMAN, PH.D., AND RANDY PETERSEN
ADAPTED FROM "STARTING OVER"

STAYING MARRIED
THROUGH TRAGEDIES

1. Commit to keeping your relationship intact.
Commitment is the foundation of relationship survival. It needs to be verbally expressed by both partners before and during a crisis.

2. Persevere.
During times of complete frustration and overwhelming despair, try to do what needs to be done next. Don't try to think ahead, just do the next thing. In time, you will feel better.

3. Respect each other's differences.
You and your partner may not handle the crisis the same way, physically or emotionally. Allow your partner to handle the crisis and heal in the way that is best for him or her.

4. Take a break.
During times of crisis, it's often helpful to find new activities to share. Doing something new together is a way of focusing your energy in a positive direction. It can also provide a temporary distraction from your emotional pain.

5. Schedule priority talk time.

If you schedule a time and stick to it, the talkative spouse knows he or she will be listened to while the more quiet spouse knows he or she only has to endure talking about the painful subject for the specified interval.

6. Avoid haggling about heavy issues in the bedroom.

Keep that a sacred place. Use any other room in the house to talk about your loss or leave the house altogether, if that's what it takes to preserve the marriage bed as a place of harmony and unity.

7. Join a support group.

Talk with others who have been through a similar experience. Try to attend meetings together, but don't force your partner to go.

8. Keep a journal.

Writing can be one of the most helpful ways for navigating a crisis. When there's no one else to listen, no one with whom you feel comfortable enough to share your deepest thoughts, your journal is ready to safely and nonjudgmentally accept whatever you say.

DON HARTING
CONDENSED FROM "MARRIAGE PARTNERSHIP" MAGAZINE

DIFFICULTIES CAN...

Deepen your faith.

Teach patience.

Develop maturity.

Build wisdom.

Force you to pray.

Remind you of what is truly important.

THE APOSTLE JAMES
ADAPTED FROM JAMES 1:2–12

TOUGH TIMES DEMAND

STRONG MINDS

GREAT HEARTS

TRUE FAITH

READY HANDS

JOSIAH GILBERT HOLLAND
JOURNALIST AND EDITOR

GETTING BACK ON TRACK

1. GET SOME OBJECTIVE COACHING FROM A THIRD PARTY.

All of us can benefit from finding a friend, pastor, or spiritual advisor who can stand back with an impartial eye and tell it to us straight. Of course, this step presupposes a willingness to act on the counsel we receive.

2. LEARN TO DREAM AGAIN.

Come to the realization that every end is also a beginning. A new dream is often an old dream that got parked on a shelf somewhere along the way.

3. SEE YOURSELF AS AN OBSTACLE TO OVERCOME.

In most situations, I am the problem. My mentalities, my pictures, and my expectations form the biggest obstacles to my success.

4. SET GOALS.

Sometimes we set ridiculous limitations by failing to set higher goals for ourselves in every area of life. When we expect more, we achieve more.

5. FIND A FOCAL POINT.

Whatever the cost, however painful the process, seeking a clear sense of purpose is the best way to keep our past from holding us back.

ED ROWELL
CONDENSED FROM "GO THE DISTANCE"

IF

IF you can keep your head when all about you panic...

IF you can stand your ground when many others doubt...

IF you can wait, and not be tired of waiting...

IF you can resist all lies and blame and hating...

IF you can dream, and not make dreams your master...

IF you can think, and not make thoughts your aim...

IF you can hear the truth when it is spoken...

IF you can humble your life when things are broken...

IF you can start again when faced with loss...

IF you can look beyond the here and now...

IF you can walk with the crowd and keep your virtue...

IF you can hold on when there is nothing in you...

IF you can fill each minute with all that it can hold...

IF you can truly care for those who hurt you...

THEN YOU WILL HAVE COME FAR, MY FRIEND.

ADAPTED FROM RUDYARD KIPLING
POET AND NOVELIST

TOUGH TIMES

WHEN OUR CHILDREN DISAPPOINT US

FACE YOUR FEARS.

If you suspect your teenager is involved in an unhealthy relationship or activity, ask about it. Talk about it. Don't be afraid to be involved in your child's life. If the situation is severe, search their room and talk to their friends. Unwelcome action may prevent unpredictable tragedy.

FACE THE TRUTH.

Sometimes a kitchen table meeting will allow family members to express feelings of injustice and hurt. Hearing the truth from those we love is not so frightening as hearing that we have been unapproachable.

SEE THE SITUATION THROUGH THEIR EYES.

It is hard for children to admit they have disappointed us. It is difficult for them to say "I was wrong." Don't berate a child. They need a noncondemning parent to talk to.

PRAYER IS ESSENTIAL.

Trust God with the outcome. Don't get in God's way. He can work effectively with our children without our telling Him how we want things done.

RECOGNIZE THAT THERE IS A POINT OF RELEASE.

A time may come when we need to free ourselves from our child for a while. A child who causes constant crisis or danger to you or other children because of unacceptable behavior may need to be placed where they can get the help needed. This is not abandonment. It is tough love.

RELINQUISH OVER AND OVER.

Sometimes the road to restoration must be paved with relinquishment and forgiveness. Even the best families are not immune to crisis, but those who arm themselves with knowledge and love will have a better rate of survival.

BARBARA BAUMGARDNER, AUTHOR, SPEAKER
CONDENSED FROM "WHEN OUR CHILDREN DISAPPOINT US"
AS PUBLISHED IN "DECISION" MAGAZINE

∽ **Listen, listen, listen.**
Be willing to listen without offering advice.

∽ **Be willing to cry with your friend.**
The greatest comfort received from a friend is not words of wisdom but tears of sorrow.

∽ **Affirm her identity.**
Often illness prevents a person from doing what she always did. She needs to be reminded that her identity lies not in what she can or can't do.

∽ **Give him time.**
A chronically ill person needs time to weep, to question, to wonder, and to grieve the loss of health. Encourage your friend to be patient with himself when accepting his limitations. It can take much longer than expected, especially if he has been healthy most of his life.

∞ Encourage.

Encourage your friend to develop new goals and expectations—to look at what he can do rather than focus on what he cannot. Also, help him grant himself permission to rest—and to cancel plans if necessary.

∞ Send healing notes.

A card saying "praying for your healing" or "hoping you feel better" or "thinking of you"—especially during a bout of more intense sickness—is a wonderful gift of hope and love.

∞ Use the power of prayer.

Let your loved one know how you are specifically praying for her, and welcome her prayer requests.

STACEY S. PADRICK
ADAPTED FROM "DISCIPLESHIP JOURNAL" MAGAZINE

HOW TO BE UNSINKABLE

1. USE WHAT YOU HAVE.

2. DON'T WORRY ABOUT WHAT YOU DON'T HAVE.

3. STAY COOL WHEN THE HEAT IS ON.

4. WHEN YOU FALL DOWN, GET UP, DUST YOURSELF OFF, AND
   KEEP GOING.

5. FOLLOW THROUGH ON YOUR DREAMS.

6. DISCIPLINE YOUR THOUGHTS.

7. FIND COMFORT IN HELPING OTHERS.

8. GIVE GOD CONTROL.

PAT WILLIAMS
CONDENSED FROM "UNSINKABLE"

WHEN LIFE IS HARD

WE ARE PRESSED ON EVERY SIDE BY TROUBLES,
but we are not crushed and broken.

WE ARE PERPLEXED,
but we don't give up and quit.

WE ARE HUNTED DOWN,
but God never abandons us.

WE GET KNOCKED DOWN,
but we get up again and keep going.

FROM 2 CORINTHIANS 4:8–9
"THE HOLY BIBLE," NLT

STEPS TO HELP A GRIEVING CHILD

1. *Give your children permission to grieve.*
   Whether the loss is the death of a family member, a major move, or the loss of a pet, your children need permission to mourn.

2. *Be available when your children are ready to grieve.*
   Being available may be the most important element in helping your children grieve. Remember, they need affection and a sense of security.

3. *Give them opportunities for creative expression.*
   Children who have difficulty verbalizing their feelings may find it easier to express them on paper. Drawing is an effective way for kids to gain control over their emotional pain and gradually deflate it.

4. *Create opportunities for play.*
   Periodically your children need to be encouraged to take a break from their grief and to play with friends. Play helps them regain a feeling of safety and security.

5. **Watch your expectations.**

   We need to be careful not to overprotect our children. Lecturing or making decisions for them is not helpful while they're coping with a loss.

6. **Make honesty a policy.**

   While grieving, our children look to us for hope and encouragement. When they ask us questions, we need to avoid giving them platitudes, and admit to them that we don't have all the answers.

7. *Allow your children to respond in their own way.*

   Don't expect your kids to respond as you do. If they begin to express strong feelings, don't block them. Allow them to cry or express anger or even bitterness.

8. *Encourage children to continue normal family routines.*

   Provide security and let kids know there are certain constants in their lives—things they can rely on to stay the same.

H. NORMAN WRIGHT
CONDENSED FROM "WILL MY LIFE EVER BE THE SAME?"

SEVEN HOLIDAY GIFTS
FOR THE GRIEVING

§ **The Gift of Hospitality**

Include a grieving friend in some of your holiday plans even if he or she has relatives nearby. Sometimes it is easier to be with people who aren't emotionally involved in your sorrow. An evening drive to see the Christmas lights or a holiday program at church can be a welcome break.

§ **The Gift of Holiday Baking**

A person who enjoys baking might tell a grieving friend that she will deliver ten dozen cookies during the week before Christmas for her to keep or give away. Twelve gift-wrapped treats with Scripture or encouraging notes attached—one to be opened each day during the twelve days before Christmas—can be fun as well as comforting for a hurting person.

§ **The Gift of a Memory**

Hope and healing often begin by recalling memories. A photo you took of the one who died, a story about something the deceased did for you, a Christmas tree ornament or a plant that can grow in a garden will all bring warm thoughts of the person no longer here.

§ **The Gift to Coax a Smile**

Grieving people need something to unwrap, a surprise, a reminder that somebody loves them. It is best if it doesn't identify with their loss in any way. Opening a gift can be a reminder that life goes on, and dreams still come true, even in the midst of heartache.

§ The Gift of Help

A homemade, hand-written coupon might be redeemable for four hours of babysitting or washing the outside windows on a sunny day. A coupon good for dinner the day after Christmas or for two hours of ironing followed by a movie can say, "I care about you. I want to help."

§ The Gift of Understanding

When people expect the grieving to forget their pain during the holidays, it is like saying the one who died never existed. Talking about memories is important that first year. The gift of a 24-hour burning candle will bring comfort during the hours when the bereaved struggles to put her grief aside. Without a word spoken, it will flicker, *I remember.*

§ The Gift of Privacy

There are times when the bereaved wants to be alone. Grown children may hesitate to leave their mother after a father dies but she needs time to be alone and cry. Even a weekend away to a warm, sunny place to bask in the sun allows for healing. Time alone can restore, refresh, and bring peace.

BARBARA BAUMGARDNER
AUTHOR OF "A PASSAGE THROUGH GRIEF: AN INTERACTIVE JOURNAL"

WHAT MADE ME STRONG

For every hill I've had to climb,

For every stone that bruised my feet,

For all the blood and sweat and grime,

For blinding storms and heat,

My heart sings but a grateful song—

These were the things that made me strong!

AUTHOR UNKNOWN

AN ATTITUDE TOWARD PAIN

EXPECT IT.

ACCEPT IT.

EMBRACE IT.

USE IT.

THOMAS A. WHITEMAN, PH.D., AND RANDY PETERSEN
FROM "STARTING OVER"

STAND UP

Fall seven times,

stand up eight.

JAPANESE PROVERB

9
Family Life

Appreciating the ups and downs together

YOU'RE MISSING THE
TRULY IMPORTANT STUFF IF...

- § the kids are startled when you want to interact with them.

- § a fun weekend for you is working at the office or working in the yard—by choice, not necessity.

- § there are many days when you don't see your kids because you're out of the house before they awake and come home after they're in bed.

- § you'd rather spend your evening on the Internet than sleeping under the stars with your child.

- § "Not now, I'm busy" is a common phrase in your home, while "Come sit down and tell me about it" is not in your vocabulary.

- § you're never off the cell phone.

- § you know the Dow Jones average but haven't a clue about your child's batting average.

- § when you say, "I'll play with you later," you actually think there will be a "later."

DAVID J. STIPECH
FROM "FOCUS ON THE FAMILY" MAGAZINE

THINGS TO REMEMBER
AS A NEW MOM

1. Be confident in your natural ability to parent.
2. Be realistic about the demands of parenting instead of letting guilt overwhelm you because you aren't perfect.
3. Accept help when it is offered.
4. Buy a good month-by-month guide to child development. These answer most of the many questions you will have.
5. Everybody has an opinion. Realize early on that you won't meet everyone's expectations.
6. Find a parenting buddy. If you can find a friend with a child the same age or a little older, you can often erase each other's worries.
7. Appreciate the moment. Instead of worrying and comparing your child to others, enjoy the specific stage your child is at—it will never be repeated.
8. When your newborn naps, use the time for a "guilty" pleasure—whether it is napping, taking a bubble bath, reading a magazine, or calling a friend.
9. Don't feel discouraged if your husband isn't as involved as you had hoped. Sometimes it takes dads a little longer to connect.
10. Find a way to record the memories. The time passes quickly and you'll appreciate looking back on those first precious months.

~~~

TANIA GRAY
HER FIRSTBORN IS TURNING ONE

WHAT I WISH I'D KNOWN

I wish I'd known...

- that children are not the central focus of a marital relationship.
- how the intensity of every emotion, when associated with a child, is magnified.
- that I didn't have to be afraid of letting go of any particular stage, period, or phase in our children's lives; each part of a child's life unfolds as a chapter in a book.
- how important traditions and memories would be for my children.
- that no two children are the same—even my own children.
- that parenting did not get easier as the children got older.
- how difficult modeling and demonstrating the proper behavior and attitude can be.
- that it would not damage my children permanently if they didn't get everything they wanted.
- that when confronted with a seemingly impossible situation with a child, all things are possible for God.
- that because of kids, my life would be an open book for everyone to share.
- that parenthood never ends.

KAY COLES JAMES
CONDENSED FROM "WHAT I WISH I'D KNOWN BEFORE I GOT MARRIED"

THREE T'S FOR YOUR FAMILY

1. TIME

Parenting takes time. Since time is finite, we must set priorities for our schedule. Carefully consider how you spend your time and whether or not you are available to your children.

2. TOUCH

You can make your children feel loved by giving them plenty of physical touch. Regular hugs, kisses, and hand-holding all say, "You are loved."

3. TALK

Tell your children your values, expectations, goals, and dreams for them, your family, and yourself. Ask them about their own worries and dreams and goals. It's not words by themselves that communicate love—it's talking with your children in a way that shows deep interest and a strong desire to be involved in their lives.

DENNIS AND BARBARA RAINEY
CONDENSED FROM "GROWING A SPIRITUALLY STRONG FAMILY"

WHAT GOOD FAMILIES
ARE DOING RIGHT

1. Strong families establish solidarity in family through rituals and traditions that belong to them.

2. Mothers and fathers model an example of a strong and loving relationship with each other.

3. Parents pattern a disciplined lifestyle and control the environment in which their children are living.

4. A loving family majors in communication. They listen to one another and respond with genuine sensitivity.

5. A family has fun! They affirm and encourage one another.

6. The family demands respect for each member of the household.

7. The family shares responsibility. Children must be taught to serve others.

8. Families have a shared religious faith. Parents teach their children virtues arising out of the common Judeo-Christian ethic.

DORTHY KELLEY PATTERSON
CONDENSED FROM "THE FAMILY"

25 WAYS TO SAY "I LOVE YOU" TO YOUR CHILD

1. Every night before bed, ask him to tell you the best and worst things about his day.

2. Reassure her that you will always keep her safe, even if scary events are happening in the world.

3. Out of nowhere, tell her that she's special, that you're proud of her, and that you feel blessed that she's yours.

4. Show him how to introduce himself to a possible new friend. Explain that though this can be scary, the payoff is big.

5. Schedule dates to hang out together—just the two of you.

6. Make eye contact whenever she talks to you.

7. Rub her back.

8. Ask for his opinion.

9. Take a spontaneous road trip to a place you know your child would like to go.

10. Tell him that he's a good kid and that you trust him.

11. Take him berry picking, and then bake a pie together.

12. Encourage her to tell you about her fears.

13. Eat dinner together.

14. Brag about her, and make sure she hears it.

15. Establish a family game night, and hold it sacred.

16. Give her the last bite of your chocolate ice cream cone.

17. Laugh hard at her knock-knock jokes, even if you've already heard them 100 times.

18. Put on your baseball glove and play catch—even if you can't catch.

19. Go for a family bike ride.

20. Rent a family movie, snuggle up on the couch, and watch it together.

21. Tell her what you like about her friends.

22. Call to say good night whenever you're away from home.

23. Treat her to a candlelit bath.

24. Send flowers or balloons to her on her birthday.

25. Say "I love you" every single day, even if it doesn't come naturally. It's never too late to start, and you'll never regret it.

RENEE BACHER
FROM "PARENTS" MAGAZINE

FAMILY LIFE

MAKING FAMILY MEALS SUCCESSFUL

⟋ **No TV!** Absolutely, positively no television during meals. This is not negotiable.

⟋ **No phone calls.** If you have an answering machine or voice mail, use it during dinner. Let friends know that calls will not be accepted during the dinner hour.

⟋ **Don't lecture or make a fuss.** Mealtime should be a pleasant time for everyone. This is not the time to reprimand the kids.

⟋ **Don't become the manners police.** Yes, we want to teach our children the proper way to eat, but family meals aren't the time to harp on what they're doing wrong.

⟋ **Make sure everyone pitches in.** Delegate chores for a week at a time, then rotate to keep things interesting.

MIMI KNIGHT
CONDENSED FROM "CHRISTIAN PARENTING TODAY" MAGAZINE

MAKING FAMILY MEALS FUN

§ **Pick good conversation starters.**
Take turns selecting a topic of conversation or placing an interesting object in the center of the table to start family discussions.

§ **Ask open-ended questions.**
Research has shown that children who are talked to and ask questions have higher IQs.

§ **Take turns.**
Just as you divide up dinnertime chores, divide up dinner-time privileges as well.

§ **Get everyone's input.**
Ask your children what would make mealtimes together more fun.

§ **Read aloud.**
Select a book that appeals to all ages. Designate a different family member every night to read for five or ten minutes as the family is finishing up the meal.

MIMI KNIGHT
CONDENSED FROM "CHRISTIAN PARENTING TODAY" MAGAZINE

SELF-ESTEEM BUILDERS

Make positive statements to each child every day.

§

Encourage children in their strengths.

§

Let children see your own mistakes and failures—nobody's perfect.

§

Allow children to solve problems on their own before you intervene.

§

Compliment children on effort, not just on final product.

BETSY CAÑAS GARMON
FROM "PARENTLIFE" MAGAZINE

RESISTING TEMPTATION

1. HELP your children understand the types of temptations they may face. Use teachable moments.

2. ENCOURAGE your kids to admit they are vulnerable to temptation. They may understand that drugs are wrong but think themselves beyond falling into such traps.

3. TEACH them to pray against temptation.

4. PROTECT your children by encouraging them to withdraw from the source of temptation.

CARLA WILLIAMS
CONDENSED FROM "FOCUS ON THE FAMILY" MAGAZINE

MANAGING CONFLICT

1. ACCEPT THAT ALL FAMILIES EXPERIENCE CONFLICT.

    Within every family there are differences of opinion, approach, style, and expression. The expectation of *no conflict* within a family is unrealistic and naive.

2. AVOID THE WORDS NEVER, EVER, AND ALWAYS.

    Such expressions are shaming and insulting. They are hurtful and do not produce the results desired.

3. SEPARATE THE BEHAVIOR FROM THE PERSON.

    Separating the behavior from the child is a powerful way to express unconditional love. Unconditional love conveys love with no strings attached regardless of the behavior. It doesn't mean you accept the behavior, but it does mean that you always accept the child as a person.

4. HAVE RULES WHICH ARE AGE-APPROPRIATE AND BE FLEXIBLE ABOUT RULE MAKING.

Many family conflicts could be eased and eliminated if parents would make the rules age-appropriate.

5. BRAINSTORM TOGETHER FOR SOLUTIONS.

Parents should involve children in seeking solutions to sources of conflict. Allowing children input develops maturity and helps them feel like a necessary part of the family unit.

6. GIVE POSITIVE FEEDBACK.

Giving positive feedback not only lets a child know that the parent notices and appreciates good behavior but is a way of balancing criticisms offered on other occasions.

VICTOR PARACHIN
CONDENSED FROM "PARENTLIFE" MAGAZINE

SQUELCHING SIBLING SQUABBLES

TRY TO TREAT YOUR CHILDREN AS SEPARATE, UNIQUE INDIVIDUALS.

Focus on each individual's style, tastes, habits, personality, and moods. This can help you understand each child better as well as help build self-esteem.

PRAISE POSITIVE BEHAVIOR.

Catch your children cooperating and getting along. Compliment them on resolving their own conflicts and helping each other.

AVOID BECOMING THE REFEREE.

Encourage children to settle their own disagreements. When possible, stay out of arguments as long as they remain verbal.

HAVE SOME FAMILY RULES.

As a family discuss the parameters of allowed behavior. Hitting, breaking things, and name-calling should not be permitted.

DISTANCE MAKES THE HEART GROW FONDER.

A time of separation will distract each person involved and allow their frustration level and emotions to cool off.

TRY TO ENJOY YOUR CHILDREN.

Parenting can be a thankless and tiresome task, especially if you feel defeated by constant sibling conflict. Realize that sibling rivalry is a normal part of childhood and do not let it steal the joy and fun that your children can bring to your life.

DEBBIE D. GREGORY
CONDENSED FROM "PARENTLIFE" MAGAZINE

HOW TO SPOT A TROUBLED CHILD

1. Has the problem continued for at least six months? Do you hear from teachers, youth advisors, and other adults that your child doesn't fit in?

2. Does your child repeatedly fight, argue, and violate the basic rights of others?

3. Do temper tantrums continue, and is disobedience an issue at home and school?

4. Are your child's poor social skills obvious when he or she participates in sports or social events?

5. Is your child uncooperative and labeled a trouble-maker?

6. Do words such as *moody* and *low self-esteem* describe your child?

7. Do you think peer pressure is forcing your child to use drugs or alcohol?

WESLEY SHARPE
FROM "HOMELIFE" MAGAZINE

SUCCESSFUL PARENTS...

See their children as gifts from God.

Understand, accept, and develop their child's bent.

Commit to leading their children to know God.

Communicate spiritual values to their children.

Exemplify godly character.

Seek to discipline their children consistently.

Spend time with their children.

ROBERT JEFFRESS
FROM "THE SOLOMON SECRETS"

12 HELPS FOR LONG-DISTANCE TRAVEL WITH CHILDREN

1. **Search the Internet** to find special children's events along your route. Let them decide which ones to take in.

2. **Pray together before starting out each day** that your trip will be safe and fun.

3. **Let them trace the trip on a map** of their own with a highlighter if they are old enough. Their very own journal can be a record of stops and points of interest for show-and-tell at school.

4. **A small, portable inflatable pool** can relieve tension and allow them to cool off in a park on a hot day.

5. **Take energy-expending items for use after a long drive:** jump ropes, bicycles, Velcro balls, Frisbees. Bad weather items can include a children's exercise video, as well as puzzles, books, and games.

6. **Explain campground or motel/hotel rules,** especially about noise and safety. If you are traveling with a dog, there are also pet rules to be observed.

7. **Participate with the children in activities;** don't just watch. Swings, miniature golf, horseshoe games, a walk, or a bike ride can all be memory makers.

8. **Identification cards must be attached to the child.** An ID card on a chain or ribbon around the neck should include make of car, color, license plate number and name of a person not on this trip to contact in case of emergency.

9. **Travel some at night with very small children** if possible. Their sleep will make driving less stressful.

10. **Describe the unfamiliar people and places they will see.** Telling some family background about relatives they will visit will help family bonding. Take lots of pictures.

11. **Stop at least once every two hours.** A stretch is good for the driver as well as the kids.

12. **Pray together at the end of each day.** Thank God for traveling safety and the gift of just being together.

BARBARA BAUMGARDNER
COLUMNIST FOR "RV COMPANION" MAGAZINE

A GREAT PARENT...

...is someone who can make the necessary personal sacrifices
to help her children feel loved, adored, and respected.

KYLE PRUETT, M.D.

...recognizes good behavior in children and
teachs them to recognize it in themselves.

SAL SEVERE, PH.D.

...makes sure that she finds the time to take care of herself,
even if it takes time away from her kids on occasion.
You don't do children any favors by always putting yourself last.

ALICE DOMAR, PH.D.

*…is a parent who keeps commitments to his children.
If he says he is going to be at their class play or baseball game,
he is always there.*

WADE HORN, PH.D., NATIONAL FATHERHOOD INSTITUTE

…is a good listener.

AITH WOHL, PRESIDENT, CHILDCARE ACTION CAMPAIGN

*…is a lifelong advocate for a child.
She is involved in every aspect of a child's life
while giving him his roots—and his wings.*

GINNY MARKELL, PRESIDENT, NATIONAL PTA

…knows that safety always comes first.

ANGELA MICKALIDE, PH.D.

COMPILED BY RON TAFFEL, PH.D.
FROM "PARENTS" MAGAZINE

SMALL GESTURES OF BIG LOVE

Surprise your child with breakfast in bed.

Plan, shop, and cook a meal together: kid's choice.

Let your child stay up a little later one night.

*Celebrate a half birthday—complete with
a half-birthday cake and presents.*

Ask your child to select music for dinner.

*Let your son or daughter sleep in your favorite T-shirt or
use your favorite mug whenever he's sick or whenever you're out of town.*

Bring your child a big bouquet of flowers.

Let your child overhear you passing on his opinion:
"I thought these print pillows wouldn't match, but Clarke noticed
how well they go with the arm chair, too."

Help your child rearrange the furniture in his room.
Bring home something new to brighten up the arrangement.

Have a double dessert night.

Take a break from Saturday chores and go kite flying.
Or go out for a round of miniature golf.

CARLY CARTER
FROM "PARENT LIFE" MAGAZINE

10
Family Lessons
Learning and maturing together

HOW TO HANDLE A BULLY

15 QUESTIONS PARENTS SHOULD ASK THEIR TEENS

QUALITIES TO BUILD IN YOUR CHILDREN

EIGHT FUN WAYS TO TEACH VALUES

30 RULES OF NEATNESS

MAXIMS OF MATURITY

WHEN YOUR CHILD WANTS TO GIVE UP

HOW TO JUGGLE FAMILY DEMANDS

WHEN YOUR CHILD OVERSTEPS BOUNDARIES

THE POWER OF CONSEQUENCES

BUILDING CAN-DO KIDS

APPRECIATING YOUR KIDS' TEACHERS

HOW YOUR KIDS CAN MAKE A POSITIVE IMPRESSION WITH TEACHERS

TEACHING KIDS ABOUT MONEY

FIVE REASONS IT'S EASIER TO SUCCEED

SEVEN STRATEGIES TO BUILD A STRONG WORK ETHIC

SEVEN IDEAS FOR YOUNG ENTREPRENEURS

HELPFUL FRIEND-FINDING TIPS

PARENTING ADVICE

HOW TO HANDLE A BULLY

Walk away

Tell them to please stop

Talk to an adult

Ask them what they want

See if they'd like to play

Share a joke with them

Ignore them

Give them a compliment

Turn them into a friend

Pray for them

DYLAN STEPHENS
AGE 11

15 QUESTIONS PARENTS SHOULD ASK THEIR TEENS

1. How often do I interrupt you when you're trying to tell me something?

2. How often do I make plans for you without asking you or consulting your schedule or preferences?

3. Do I trust you? If not, is there a reason?

4. How do you feel when I lecture you?

5. Do I talk to you like you're a little kid?

6. Do I try to cheer you up every time you are sad or feel bad?

7. If you are upset, do I act like what you are feeling is important?

8. Can you tell me when you're sad, angry, or depressed?

9. Is there anything you can't talk about with me? Why?

10. Do you feel like I understand what you are trying to say?

11. Do I get angry if you disagree with me?

12. Do I criticize you? If so, what about?

13. Is there anything you want to ask me but are afraid to ask?

14. Do you trust me?

15. What could I do so that you could trust me more?

HARON HERSH
ADAPTED FROM "MOM, I FEEL FAT!"

QUALITIES TO BUILD
IN YOUR CHILDREN

Hard work—doing his part with zest.

Efficient—getting the job done quickly and well.

A good communicator—listening well to instructions and having good input.

Responsible—doing what is right without constant supervision.

A self-starter—seeing what needs to be done and doing it.

A good time manager—punctual, doesn't procrastinate.

Smart about practicalities—learning what things work and what things don't.

Respectful of self—thinking he deserves to live a well-ordered life.

Respectful of others—thinking of what others want and need.

Thoughtful and caring—doing more than his share when the situation requires it.

A good team member—working well with others in every way.

Fair—not burdening others with his things or jobs.

Positive toward work—having a healthy "can do" mind-set.

Self-controlled—saying yes or no to his wants as appropriate.

SANDRA FELTON
FROM "NEAT MOM, MESSIE KIDS"

EIGHT FUN WAYS TO TEACH VALUES

1.
HAVE A TAG SALE.

Ask your child to help you round up old toys, books, and clothing. Explain that it's good to sell items you no longer need to people who do.

2.
ADOPT A GRANDPARENT.

Make friends with an elderly person in your community. Find ways to brighten her day or lighten her load. Bake your new friend a batch of brownies. Offer to shovel the snow off her walks or pick up her groceries.

3.
MAKE A CHORE CHART.

Teach responsibility by having your child take on a few important daily jobs, such as feeding the fish and setting the table. List his chores across the top of a page and the days of the week down the side.

4.
DO SECRET GOOD DEEDS.

Plan a day when each member of your family does something special for another member on the sly.

5.

NEATEN UP THE NEIGHBORHOOD.

Find a littered playground or a vacant lot that's in need of some TLC, and take it upon yourselves to spiff it up.

6.

PLAY THE GRATITUDE GAME.

The next time you're riding in the car, play the "ABCs of thankfulness." Take turns naming things you feel grateful for that begin with the letters *A, B, C,* and so on.

7.

DESIGN "GET WELL" PILLOWCASES.

Ask your child how he would feel if he were sick and received a special gift. Then suggest using colorful fabric paints or markers to decorate plain pillowcases, and deliver them to the pediatric floor of a local hospital.

8.

CREATE A FAMILY TIME LINE.

Draw a line down the length of butcher paper. At one end, mark the day you met or married your spouse. Add other events, such as a birth, a move, or the day your child started preschool, and continue until the present.

PAMELA KRAMER
CONDENSED FROM "PARENTS" MAGAZINE

30 RULES OF NEATNESS

In our family...

We clear the table and clean the kitchen together.

We hang up the towels neatly after bathing.

We put what we need to take to school or work the next day by the front door the night before.

We don't drop our things when we come in the door. We put them where they belong.

We put dirty clothes into the hamper as soon as we take them off.

We put things back where they belong as soon as we finish with them.

We make our beds before we leave our room in the morning.

We put dirty dishes in the dishwasher, not in the sink.

We take responsibility for completing the chores assigned to us.

We don't complain about our responsibilities.

We always flush the toilet immediately after using it.

We put away toys, games, tools, and stuff immediately after finishing with them.

We don't leave things out just because we plan to get back to the project later.

We wash, dry, fold, and put away our clothes as one continuous job.

We make sure all trash goes into the trash basket.

We value each other and the contribution each makes.

We keep our closets and drawers neat.

We use the team concept. Each person does his or her part to support all.

We are willing to help others where necessary because we are a team.

We don't make messes or create work for others.

We don't boss others. We focus on our own responsibilities.

We speak kindly to each other.

We try to think ahead to solve problems before they happen.

We pay attention to maintaining beauty.

We push our chairs up to the table when we get up from it.

We use one bath towel for a week.

We strive to complete projects and clean up expeditiously.

The person who uses the last sheet of toilet paper puts a new roll on the roller.

We make a list on the white board of what we need from the store.

We move the garbage cans out of sight after they are emptied from the curb.

SANDRA FELTON
CONDENSED FROM "NEAT MOM, MESSIE KIDS"

§ *Responsibility begins in small things.* It's never too early—or too late—to expect your children to manage small responsibilities. Encourage your children to help out around the house, even if it initially creates more work for you; chores are the perfect training ground for a healthy work ethic.

§ *Getting along with others begins at home.* There is no better place for teaching conflict resolution than the home. You can also teach your children how to get along with others by having family rules and seeing that every family member follows them.

§ *Everyone lives somewhere—and everyone needs to take care of that somewhere.* Home should be a place to nourish ourselves and others. Make activities such as shopping, laundry, and cleaning a part of your children's everyday life.

§ *Getting along in a great big and sometimes uncertain world requires life navigation skills.* These include everything from learning to read a map to knowing the proper way to answer the telephone.

§ *Things break and need maintenance.* Children learn home maintenance and repair skills by spending time alongside mom and dad as you take care of the house. The more you teach them, the more self-reliant they'll be when they leave home.

§ *Much of life involves money; either we learn to handle it or it will handle us.* Teaching children the value of money must be intentional. You can teach them comparison shopping and wise consumerism by taking them shopping with you.

§ *Each of us has only one body; we have to take care of it.* Healthy bodies and healthy minds go hand in hand. Children need to know what's good for their bodies.

§ *Our brains are valuable things; we must learn to make them work at peak performance.* A healthy mind is one that learns effectively. Uncovering your children's learning styles and helping them learn effective study methods for those styles will improve their learning potential.

§ *The more decisions we make, the better decision makers we are.* Encourage your children to make small decisions from an early age. As they grow older and life becomes more complicated, teach them to list their priorities and think about the pros and cons of any decision.

§ *Life is a creative exercise; we need to develop and nourish our creativity.* Whether your children end up artists or accountants, they will need to be creative. By instilling an appreciation for creative skills, we will give our children an outlet for creative expression and a chance to contribute something beautiful and personal to the world.

CHRISTINE M. FIELD
CONDENSED FROM "HELP FOR THE HARRIED HOMESCHOOLER"

WHEN YOUR CHILD WANTS
TO GIVE UP

1. **Examine your expectations.**

   While expecting the best from your child, you need to make sure that you are not expecting more than your child can realistically deliver.

2. **Emphasize effort and perseverance instead of performance.**

   After all, it is not the grade or outcome that counts as much as the effort. Success is not usually the result of undisciplined raw ability but of moderate ability paired with perseverance.

3. **Give your child a model of how to respond to difficult situations in a positive way.**

   Your child will learn to cope with difficult situations more easily if he can see real-life examples of you doing the same.

4. **Ask yourself why.**

   Children who have difficulty responding to failure often tend to assume that the failure is due to something wrong with them. Together with your child, gently examine his "failed" experiences, asking him why he thinks they happened. See what possible reasons he can think of, and together identify the reasons that seem to best fit his situation.

5. *Straight thinking is as important for your child as a straight arrow is in an archery contest.*
    Just as a crooked arrow could mean defeat for the archer, thoughts that miss the mark can spell disaster for your child when the going gets tough. Help your child develop a set of thoughts that will promote a positive attitude and perseverance.

6. *Safe practice.*
    Your child needs to practice in a safe setting, where he can develop his skills at his own pace. Make sure to give him lots of positive encouragement for his effort and for being brave enough to risk learning something new. Once your child has begun to develop his skill, encourage him to gradually use his new skills in other situations, going only as fast as he feels comfortable.

DR. TODD CARTMELL
CONDENSED FROM "THE PARENT SURVIVAL GUIDE"

HOW TO JUGGLE FAMILY DEMANDS

Just say no.
Learn to say some no's when you're making up the family schedule.

Use your attitude for good and not evil.
There's power in your attitude. If your disposition stinks, your kids will pick up on that—and mimic it.

Go fish for good times.
Fish "quality" time out of the schedule where you can. Even time in the car can become an enjoyable time to chat.

Get down and get goofy.
Don't spare the clowning around. It's easy to take life too seriously and miss out on some great laughs when you're feeling overwhelmed.

Let bedtime be bedlam.
Kids are most ready to share with you later in the evening. They'll do anything to drag out bedtime and stay up a little later—even talk with a parent about what's going on in their lives.

Expect super success, but not super powers.
Remember that when we make mistakes but handle them correctly and humbly, we can teach our children even more than if we had done it the "Super Parent" way in the first place.

RHONDA RHEA
CONDENSED FROM THE "ST. LOUIS FAMILY GAZETTE"

WHEN YOUR CHILD
OVERSTEPS BOUNDARIES

Stay calm.

Gather information.

Talk to them/listen to them.

Share your concerns.

Explain the repercussions and
rewards of their behavior.

Connect with other parents
and resources for perspective.

Set clear consequences.

Follow through with those consequences.

Give positive direction and
encouragement for the future.

Affirm your love.

JUNE HUNT
AUTHOR AND RADIO PERSONALITY

THE POWER OF CONSEQUENCES

1. GET SMART ABOUT CHILD DEVELOPMENT
    For consequences to mean something to your children, you need to know what your child can and can't understand. You can read about child development, observe other kids, ask seasoned parents for advice, or find a mentor to figure out what your child is ready for.

2. MAKE SURE THE TIME IS RIGHT
    The sooner you practice allowing your child to experience logical consequences, the better for all.

3. SET CLEAR EXPECTATIONS
    For children to learn from consequences, parents need to make sure children know exactly what behaviors are acceptable and what the results will be for misbehavior. Provide simple, straightforward expectations so that even a young child can understand.

4. MAKE LOGICAL CONNECTIONS
    The whole idea behind logical consequences is that the consequence is a clear, natural result of the behavior.

5. DON'T BE A RESCUER

Naturally, parents want to protect their children from unhappiness. But when we start excusing them from their homework, driving to drop things off at school, or paying their speeding tickets, we aren't doing them any favors.

6. BE WILLING TO GET TOUGH

Independence and responsibility go hand in hand. You can't give one without the other.

7. USE POSITIVE CONSEQUENCES, TOO

Consequences don't have to be negative. Research has shown that people learn faster when they are rewarded for their behavior than when the outcome is unpleasant.

SUZANNE WOODS FISHER
CONDENSED FROM "CHRISTIAN PARENTING TODAY"

BUILDING CAN-DO KIDS

1. **Be empathetic.**
   Continually stop and think about how you'd feel if someone said to you the same things you're saying to your children.

2. **Communicate with respect.**
   Always consider whether you're saying things in a way that will make your children more receptive.

3. **Be flexible.**
   Parents want their children to be adaptable, thoughtful, and receptive to new ideas, but they often fail to model these behaviors.

4. **Give undivided attention.**
   Kids feel loved when they know their parents enjoy being with them. Schedule a special time—even if it's only 15 minutes daily—to give each of your children undivided attention.

5. **Accept your kids for who they are.**
   Your children may not match your expectations, but it's vital to recognize their innate temperaments. When kids feel appreciated for who they are, they'll feel more secure reaching out to others and learning how to solve problems.

6. **Give kids a chance to contribute.**
   When we enlist children in helping others, we communicate our faith in their ability to handle a variety of tasks and give them a sense of responsibility.

7. **Treat mistakes as learning experiences.**
   Kids whose parents overreact to mistakes tend to avoid taking risks and end up blaming others for their problems.

8. **Emphasize your children's strengths.**
   Although resilient kids aren't deterred by failure, they also relish their successes. Their sense of accomplishment and pride gives them the confidence to persevere the next time they face a challenge.

9. **Let your kids solve problems and make decisions.**
   One trap that many parents fall into is the tendency to rescue their children too quickly.

10. **Discipline to teach.**
    The true meaning of the word *discipline* is "to teach." The ultimate goal is to nurture self-discipline so that your children will act responsibly even when you aren't around.

ROBERT BROOKS, PH.D., AND SAM GOLDSTEIN, PH.D.
CONDENSED FROM "RAISING RESILIENT CHILDREN" AS PRINTED IN "PARENTS" MAGAZINE

FAMILY LESSONS

Write notes of gratitude.

There are plenty of parents who criticize. You be the one to encourage.

Volunteer in the classroom.

Even if you can only volunteer one hour a week, it gives much-needed relief to a teacher.

Attend back-to-school night.

Whatever your school calls it, attend meetings where you visit your child's classroom and meet his teacher.

Help your child write a note.

Ask your children what they like most about a teacher and then help them put their words on paper.

Letter to the newspaper.
Write a letter to the editor of your newspaper and mention specific accomplishments of a school or school program.

Give a keepsake gift.
Consider giving a book to a favorite teacher and writing an inscription on the first page. Be sure to date the inscription.

Donate to the school library.
Donate a great new book to the school library and write inside that it is given in appreciation of a certain teacher.

Pray often.
A good teacher can change the course of a child's life, but this awesome task needs the encouragement of parents who pray.

ALICE GRAY
COMPILER OF "STORIES FOR A TEACHER'S HEART"

HOW YOUR KIDS CAN MAKE A POSITIVE IMPRESSION WITH TEACHERS

Develop relationships.
Simply saying hello to teachers in the hallway helps.

Use active body language.
Eye contact and nodding shows that students are listening.

Be aware of timing.
Have students approach teachers for help at a convenient time, not when they are trying to get class started or helping another student.

Be positive.
When students have teachers they appreciate, they should let the teachers know. If a particular lesson interests them, encourage students to make it known.

Respond.

When questions are posed or a discussion started, students should get involved. Involvement will be rewarded.

Show effort.

Again, even if they aren't confident and skilled in a particular area, teachers will notice and appreciate their effort.

Remember that teachers are human.

Like all of us, teachers have good days and bad days, and it helps when students are aware of that.

TANIA GRAY
HIGH SCHOOL TEACHER AND NATIONAL HONOR SOCIETY ADVISOR

TEACHING KIDS ABOUT MONEY

BE A ROLE MODEL—Kids are quick to pick up their parents' attitudes toward money. Track your own spending habits for a month, then determine how much of your money is going to wants as opposed to needs.

TALK ABOUT MONEY, A LOT—Discuss finances with your kids, even if they seem too young to understand the finer points. Don't be afraid to admit the mistakes you've made in your own life.

TURN OFF THE TV—You can't isolate your kids completely from all the cool gadgets begging for their attention, but you can keep the sales pitches out of your home, and this is one way to do it.

SHOP WITH YOUR KIDS—Use your weekly trip to the grocery store as an object lesson. Before you go, have the kids clip coupons and help write the grocery list. Once you're at the store, talk to them about the purchases you make. Compare the prices, quantities, and value of each item and work together to make wise purchases.

TAKE ADVANTAGE OF SPECIAL OCCASIONS—If your son has been begging for the latest Nintendo game or designer jeans, have him add it to his birthday or Christmas list. This way, he appreciates the item more and learns a lesson in patience as well.

GIVE THEM A JOB—Even small jobs—setting the table, mowing the lawn, or keeping their rooms clean—give kids a sense of pride, self-discipline, and work ethic.

SET LIMITS—If your daughter needs a new pair of jeans, decide on an amount that you feel is reasonable for the purchase. If they cost more, require her to earn the difference. This puts the power in her hands. She has to decide if the jeans are really worth the extra work and cash.

GIVE A LITTLE CASH—Once your kids reach fourth or fifth grade, you can let them start making some of their own financial decisions. Have your children make a list of things they need (and want). Then "give" your kids a certain amount and talk about the best way to spend the money and still get the essentials.

TEACH THEM TO TITHE THEIR MONEY...—Encourage your children to give 10 percent of their allowance or job earnings. That doesn't necessarily mean it has to go into the offering plate. Help them sponsor a child, buy supplies for a food pantry, or purchase small toys to send to needy children at Christmas.

...AND THEIR TIME—Get the whole family involved in community outreach. Deliver food baskets, clean up litter in your neighborhood, or spend some time at a local nursing home or homeless shelter. As your children learn to contribute to their community, they'll also learn lessons in compassion, gratitude, and selflessness.

LISA JACKSON
ADAPTED FROM "CHRISTIAN PARENTING TODAY"

SEVEN STRATEGIES TO
BUILD A STRONG WORK ETHIC

1. START EARLY.

The groundwork is laid well before kindergarten. The children who have the opportunity to serve when they want to will be more likely to step up to a task later on.

2. ACCEPT WHAT YOU GET.

Naturally, letting a four-year-old mop the floor means your floor won't get very clean. Still, it's important that we graciously praise the effort and the desire to help, not the results.

3. KNOW YOUR CHILDREN.

Children are individuals and mature at different rates. As your child takes on new chores and responsibilities, strike a balance between accepting his best effort and raising the bar to challenge him.

4. TEACH DELAYED GRATIFICATION.

It takes a proactive approach to help your child develop thoughtfulness and self-control—two traits that will be essential for avoiding the temptations of the teen years. It starts by establishing a pattern: We work and then we play.

5. EQUIP THEM TO EARN.

Help your kids find work they'll enjoy, and you won't have to push them out the door to do it. You'll undoubtedly have to offer a little work of your own to get them started.

6. ENCOURAGE VOLUNTEERING.

Teaching a child to enjoy working for money is a good thing, but teaching him to enjoy service for its own sake is best.

7. BE A ROLE MODEL.

So much of who our children turn out to be is a reflection, not of what we try to pour into them, but of what they see in us.

BARBARA CURTIS
CONDENSED FROM "CHRISTIAN PARENTING TODAY"

SEVEN IDEAS FOR
YOUNG ENTREPRENEURS

1. Allow your kids to take part in your next family garage sale. Let them help pare down the toy surplus and keep the profit.

2. Look for bargains at flea markets or estate sales that older kids can buy and resell. With some elbow grease and paint, an old bike or piece of furniture can fetch a good price. Collectibles can also be valuable finds.

3. Pet sitting is always a welcome service to neighbors and friends who travel. Young children can learn pet care as well as make a few dollars keeping a hamster for a week.

4. Those who are old enough to operate an oven can make and sell baked goods to friends and family. Hire them to make the cake for the next birthday. Figuring the cost of ingredients is also a valuable tool. You may find a market for nutritious snacks.

5. Giving an offering is also part of receiving. Let children give of their time to help an older neighbor or your church with lawn care or other jobs. In this case let God be the paymaster.

6. You can invest in their gifts and talents by commissioning and purchasing a work of art to frame and hang in your home. Hire your young musician to play for a set amount of time at your next party.

7. Teach kids how their money can work for them. Let them choose one share of stock to buy with part of their investment money and then watch the paper as the price changes.

ROBIN POPP
FROM "HOMELIFE" MAGAZINE

HELPFUL FRIEND-FINDING TIPS

Be willing to have kids over to your house. Get to know the children your kids are drawn to. Watch them interact with each other and discern whether the interaction is healthy or destructive.

Be available for your kids when they get home from school. That's when you'll get the most details about the people they came in contact with that day.

Constantly remind your kids how important they are. When they blow it, put your hands on their shoulders, look them in the eye, and say, "You are too important to be making those kinds of choices."

Don't be afraid to say no to them if they're drawn to someone who could be dangerous.

SUSIE LARSON
CONDENSED FROM "FOCUS ON THE FAMILY" MAGAZINE

PARENTING ADVICE

1. Children need a regular routine in daily life.

2. Parents must first conquer the will in order to fashion the minds of their children.

3. Children can be taught early to ask politely for what they want.

4. A child found guilty of wrong doing should not be punished if he confessed to his wrong and promised to amend.

5. No act such as lying, pilfering, disobedience, or quarreling should be permitted to pass unpunished.

6. A child should not be punished twice for the same act of disobedience.

7. Acts of obedience ought to be rewarded frequently.

8. In anything done to please, though the performance may not be well, the child should be tenderly directed how to do better.

9. A child must be taught rights of property belonging to self and others.

10. A child must be taught that promises are to be strictly observed.

SUSANNAH WESLEY
18TH-CENTURY MOTHER OF NINE

11
Wisdom

Learning from the experiences of others

TEN THINGS THAT REALLY MATTER

1.
Always tell the truth.

2.
Be sure you have all the facts before making a decision.

3.
Keep open and friendly relations with God, family, and neighbors.

4.
Devote time to helping others.

5.
Review and adjust personal priorities on a regular basis.

6.
Be financially responsible.

7.
Discover "blind spots" by seeking advice from others.

8.
Make personal hygiene a priority.

9.
Become interdependent—we really do need each other.

10.
Recognize God in daily life and explore the power of prayer.

DR. JOSEPH C. ALDRICH
PRESIDENT EMERITUS, MULTNOMAH BIBLE COLLEGE AND SEMINARY

WHEN NOT TO OPEN YOUR MOUTH

When you're in the heat of anger.

When you don't have all the facts.

When it is time to listen.

When you are tempted to joke about sin.

When you would be ashamed of your words later.

When your words might convey the wrong impression.

When the issue is none of your business.

When you are tempted to tell an outright lie.

When your words will damage someone else's reputation.

When your words might hurt a friendship.

When you may have to eat your words later.

When you have already said too much.

When you have promised to keep a confidence.

When you tend to talk before thinking.

When your words stir up dissension.

When you are tempted to praise yourself.

ADAPTED FROM THE BOOK OF PROVERBS
"THE HOLY BIBLE"

WISDOM

Someone who has lived longer than you.
When you're young, find someone who has lived twice as long. When you are more mature, find someone who has lived at least a decade longer.

Someone who has experienced a similar challenge.
Connect with one who has experienced your difficulty and has learned how to conquer it in a meaningful way.

The book of Proverbs in the Bible.
There are 31 practical chapters in this book full of great advice. Read one chapter each day and then apply as much as you can.

Someone who is considered an expert in the field.
Seek out a person who has researched, studied, explored, and practiced the information you're interested in.

Someone who knows you well and cares deeply for you.
There is no replacement for someone who knows your strengths and weaknesses, your history and goals, your loves and frustrations.

Autobiographies of great people.
Powerful lessons can be learned from the lives of those who have made significant marks on history.

Someone whom you respect.
Spend time with a person you regard as wise, compassionate, successful, virtuous, or trustworthy.

Sincere and faithful prayers.
Maybe God has not given you direction because you have not yet asked.

ROBERT BOBOSKY
A SUCCESSFUL ENTREPRENEUR

PRINCIPLE 1
You shall not worry, for worry is the most unproductive of all human activities.

PRINCIPLE 2
You shall not be fearful, for most of the things we fear never come to pass.

PRINCIPLE 3
You shall not cross bridges before you come to them, for no one yet has succeeded in accomplishing this.

PRINCIPLE 4
You shall face each problem as it comes. You can only handle one at a time anyway.

PRINCIPLE 5
You shall not take problems to bed with you, for they make very poor bedfellows.

PRINCIPLE 6
You shall not borrow other people's problems. They can better care for them than you can.

PRINCIPLE 7

You shall not try to relive yesterday for good or ill; it is forever gone. Concentrate on what is happening in your life and be happy now.

PRINCIPLE 8

You shall be a good listener, for only when you listen do you hear ideas different from your own.

PRINCIPLE 9

You shall not become "bogged down" by frustration, for 90 percent of it is rooted in self-pity and will only interfere with positive action.

PRINCIPLE 10

You shall count your blessings and never overlook small ones, for a lot of small blessings add up to a big one.

AUTHOR UNKNOWN
CONDENSED FROM "DARE TO TRUST, DARE TO HOPE AGAIN"

WORDS OF WISDOM

∞ People do not grow old. When they cease to grow, they become old.

∞ You cannot do a kindness too soon, for you never know how soon it will be too late.

∞ It is a happy talent to know how to play.

∞ Great men are they who see that the spiritual is stronger than any material force.

∞ People only see what they are prepared to see.

∞ We ask for long life, but 'tis deep life, or grand moments, that signify.

∞ The invariable mark of wisdom is to see the miraculous in the common.

∞ The excellent is new forever.

∞ A man is what he thinks about all day long.

∞ Many eyes go through the meadow, but few see the flowers in it.

∞ Be an opener of doors.

∞ No man ever prayed heartily, without learning something.

∞ Do not go where the path may lead, go instead where there is no path and leave a trail.

∞ For everything you miss, you gain something else, and for everything you gain, you lose something else.

∞ What lies behind us and what lies before us are tiny matters compared to what lies within us.

∞ The world is all gates, all opportunities, strings of tension waiting to be struck.

RALPH WALDO EMERSON
POET AND ESSAYIST

WISDOM

Eyes that look are common, eyes that see are rare.

J. OSWALD SANDERS

Wisdom is knowing what to do next; virtue is doing it.

DAVID STAR JORDAN

In matters of principle, stand like a rock.
In matters of taste, swim with the current.

THOMAS JEFFERSON

He is no fool who gives what he cannot keep
to gain what he cannot lose.

JIM ELLIOT

It is well for one to know more than he says.

TITUS MARCIUS PLAUTUS

If one does not know to which harbor he's headed,
there is no such thing as a good wind.

SENECA

The wise learn many things from their enemies.

ARISTOPHANES

My basic principle is that you don't make decisions because
they are easy…cheap…popular; you
make them because they're right.

THEODORE HESBURGH

Concern yourself not with your failures, but
with all that is still possible for you to do.

POPE JOHN XXIII

A life of wisdom…involves simplicity, independence,
magnanimity, and trust.

HENRY DAVID THOREAU

Make the most of the best and the least of the worst.

ROBERT LOUIS STEVENSON

There are only two ways to live your life:
One is as though nothing is a miracle;
the other is as though everything is a miracle.

ALBERT EINSTEIN

A heart at peace gives life to the body.

KING SOLOMON

TEN WAYS TO SPEAK THE TRUTH

1. CONSISTENTLY
   Speak truth in good times and bad.

2. COMPLETELY
   Speak the truth and nothing but the truth.

3. CLEARLY
   Speak truth so that understanding is promoted.

4. COMPASSIONATELY
   Speak the truth in love.

5. CAREFULLY
   Speak truth with tact and wisdom.

6. CONSTRUCTIVELY
   Speak the truth so as to encourage and build up others.

7. COURAGEOUSLY
   Speak truth without fear of personal cost or discomfort.

8. CONFIDENTLY
   Speak the truth knowing that honesty is the best policy.

9. CONTRITELY
   Speak truth in a humble way.

10. CEASELESSLY
    Speak the truth until the end of life.

DR. STEVE STEPHENS
PSYCHOLOGIST AND SEMINAR SPEAKER

THE MORE YOU HAVE

THE MORE YOU HAVE, the more you want.

THE MORE YOU HAVE, the less you're satisfied.

THE MORE YOU HAVE, the more people will come after it.

THE MORE YOU HAVE, the more you realize it does you no good.

THE MORE YOU HAVE, the more you have to worry about.

THE MORE YOU HAVE, the more you can hurt yourself by holding on to it.

THE MORE YOU HAVE, the more you have to lose.

THE MORE YOU HAVE, the more you'll leave behind.

RANDY ALCORN
CONDENSED FROM "THE TREASURE PRINCIPLE"

DON'T LET MONEY CONTROL YOU

1. Determine What Matters Most

History is full of stories of people who made it big but failed to make it good. You don't have to follow in their footsteps. You can learn from their life lessons.

2. Learn That Wealth Is Not the Answer

Once you've achieved a certain number of possessions, you begin to realize that one more is not going to do it. Then you become ripe for something meaningful.

3. Seek Financial Wisdom

If you want to learn about budgeting, investments, and fiscal management, you will have to take the initiative yourself to learn. Living within your means is a major key to enjoying your wealth without becoming materialistic and bound by debt and the need for more. Money has a way of creating an appetite for more that is rarely satiated.

4. Give Away Your Resources

Perhaps the greatest proof that money does not have you in its grip is if you are giving it away to good causes. Money tends to most closely represent the seat of priorities. It is not until our priorities change and money loses its grip on us that we are able to become spiritually mature.

ALAN NELSON
CONDENSED FROM "MY OWN WORST ENEMY"

TIPS FOR SMART LIVING

1. Open your door and heart to those who don't have as much as you do.

2. Find the good in every situation even when there doesn't seem to be any.

3. Act like a kid every now and then.

4. Think of things you'd like to accomplish in the next 10, 20, or 30 years.

5. Go away for a weekend with your best friends. You'll come back with a big smile and a great attitude.

6. Do something special for yourself that you've always wanted to do.

7. Get a pet and love it. Watch what it gives back to you.

8. Take your vitamins.

9. Treasure your family and friends. Appreciate them for who they are and expect nothing in return.

10. Never accept that this is the way it has to be. Only you can make it happen! Start now.

11. Never think you are too old.

12. Live, laugh, and enjoy.

DEBRA-LEE S. LEVESQUE
LOVER OF LIFE

THINGS I'VE LEARNED LATELY

- Life is short and death unthwartable.

- You should never wait to tell someone why you love them.

- People are precious.

- Relationships take work.

- You really have to accept people as they are and not try to change them into what you think they should be.

- Midnight laughter cleanses you.

- Coincidences are really "God things."

- Love always trusts, always hopes.

- You don't have to know everything.

- Work is necessary.

- We all struggle—no one is as confident as he seems.

- Sometimes you have to let people go.

- Change is inevitable.

- What a person sees in you is sometimes very different from what you think he's seeing.

DANAE JACOBSON, AGE 16
ADAPTED FROM "THINGS I'VE LEARNED LATELY"

THE BETTER WAY

Excellence is willing to be wrong,
Perfection is being right.

Excellence is risk,
Perfection is fear.

Excellence is powerful,
Perfection is anger and frustration.

Excellence is spontaneous,
Perfection is control.

Excellence is accepting,
Perfection is judgment.

Excellence is giving,
Perfection is taking.

Excellence is confident,
Perfection is doubt.

Excellence is flowing,
Perfection is pressure.

Excellence is journey,
Perfection is destination.

AUTHOR UNKNOWN

WHEN MAKING YOUR DECISIONS

1.
*Make your decisions based upon the timeless
and proven principles given in the Bible.*

2.
Make decisions that show virtue.

3.
Make decisions that promote truth and integrity.

4.
Make decisions that you would admire and respect if made by others.

5.
*Make decisions that you would like to have your children
and grandchildren emulate.*

CHARLES CRISMIER
ADAPTED FROM "RENEWING THE SOUL OF AMERICA"

12 POWERFUL WORDS

1. The most bitter—*hate*

2. The most tragic—*unforgiven*

3. The most treasured—*love*

4. The most encouraging—*friend*

5. The most cruel—*revenge*

6. The most enduring—*faith*

7. The most painful—*alone*

8. The most comforting—*hope*

9. The most difficult—*discipline*

10. The most beautiful—*grace*

11. The most admired—*humility*

12. The most awesome—*God*

JOHN VAN DIEST
ASSOCIATE PUBLISHER

BEWARE OF...

rest leading to laziness.

carefulness leading to fear.

anger leading to abuse.

confidence leading to pride.

self-care leading to selfishness.

enjoyment leading to addiction.

gentleness leading to weakness.

freedom leading to lack of discipline.

leadership leading to dominance.

courage leading to foolhardiness.

~~~

DR. STEVE STEPHENS
PSYCHOLOGIST AND SEMINAR SPEAKER

WHAT YOU DESERVE

§

Justice is…
getting what you deserve.

§

Mercy is…
not getting what you deserve.

§

Grace is…
getting what you don't deserve.

H. DALE BURKE
PASTOR, COUNSELOR, AND CONFERENCE SPEAKER

VISION

A vision without a task is but a dream,

a task without vision is drudgery,

a vision with a task is the hope of the world.

AUTHOR UNKNOWN
ON THE CORNERSTONE OF A CHURCH IN ENGLAND, DATED 1730

12
Faith

Discovering the source of joy and peace

WHAT GOD GIVES

For despair,   *He gives hope.*

For fear,   *He gives courage.*

For anxiety,   *He gives peace.*

For rejection,   *He gives acceptance.*

For loneliness,   *He gives love.*

For frustration,   *He gives encouragement.*

For failure,   *He gives forgiveness.*

For bondage,   *He gives freedom.*

For dishonesty,   *He gives truth.*

For confusion,   *He gives order.*

For pain,   *He gives comfort.*

For emptiness,   *He gives purpose.*

For sadness,   *He gives joy.*

For darkness,   *He gives light.*

For death,   *He gives eternal life.*

DR. STEVE STEPHENS
PSYCHOLOGIST AND SEMINAR SPEAKER

FIVE KINDS OF GOD MOMENTS

1. *Amazing Rescue*
   A moment when God guarded you, healed you, rescued you, or made a way out for you.

2. *Holy Attraction*
   A moment when God led you toward a healthier path, enabled you to resist a temptation, or inspired you to take the high road.

3. *Unearned Blessing*
   A moment when God gave you an unexpected blessing or an undeserved gift.

4. *Revealed Truth*
   A moment when God spoke to you through the Bible, inner peace, wise counsel, or a God-inspired message.

5. *Valuable Adversity*
   A moment in which God sustained you in a difficult time or made you stronger through the test of adversity.

ALAN D. WRIGHT
FROM "THE GOD MOMENT PRINCIPLE"

UNDERSTANDING HOPE

Hope works when riches fail.

Hope causes us to trust God's promises.

Hope looks beyond today's crushing problems.

Hope gives the farmer courage to plant, cultivate, and harvest.

Hope waits for spring when in the midst of the harshest winter.

Hope believes that eternal life exists beyond the grave.

Hope keeps company with faith and love.

Hope is the reason we pray.

CHARLES B. DARLAND
RETIRED COLLEGE PROFESSOR

FAITH

WHEN YOU TRUST GOD

There's no barrier too high,

No valley too deep,

No dream too extreme,

No challenge too great.

CHARLES SWINDOLL
FROM "STRENGTHENING YOUR GRIP"

GOD SHALL BE...

My hope,

My stay,

My guide,

And lantern to my feet.

WILLIAM SHAKESPEARE
POET AND PLAYWRIGHT

PRAYER IS...

...the mightiest of all weapons that created natures can wield.
MARTIN LUTHER

❧

...reaching out after the unseen.
ANDREW MURRAY

❧

...not preparation for the battle; it is the battle.
OSWALD CHAMBERS

❧

...the acid test of devotion.
SAMUEL CHADWICK

❧

...the mother of a thousand blessings.
JOHN CHRYSOSTROM

...a dialogue between two people who love each other.

ROSALIND RINKER

...life passionately wanting, wishing, desiring God's triumph.

—GEORGE CAMPBELL MORGAN

...knocking at the door; faith is the expectation that it will be opened.

W. J. HARNEY

...hemming in your day so it is unlikely to unravel.

AUTHOR UNKNOWN

...a path to God's blessing.

BRUCE WILKINSON

WHAT FAITH IS

§ Doing the right thing regardless of the consequences and knowing God will turn the ultimate effect to good.

§ Reliance on the certainty that God has a pattern for my life when everything seems meaningless.

§ Confidence that God is acting for my highest good when He says no to my prayers.

§ Realizing that I am useful to God not in spite of my scars but because of them.

§ Accepting the fact that God knows better than I do what is ultimately good for me.

§ Living with the unexplained.

§ The way to please God.

PAMELA REEVE
FROM "FAITH IS..."

WHAT FAITH DOES

§ Faith looks for the good in yourself and others instead of harping on the worst.

§ Faith opens doors where despair slams them shut.

§ Faith discovers what can be done instead of grumbling about what cannot.

§ Faith creates flashes of light instead of cursing the darkness.

§ Faith regards problems, small and large, as opportunities.

§ Faith cherishes no illusions, nor does it yield to the temptation of cynicism.

§ Faith sets big goals and is not frustrated by repeated challenges or setbacks.

§ Faith pushes ahead when it would be easy to quit.

§ Faith puts up with modest gains, realizing that the longest journey begins with a single, unfaltering step.

§ Faith accepts misunderstandings and even confusion as the price for serving the greater good of others.

§ Faith is a good loser because it has the divine assurance of victory.

GREGORY JANTZ
CONDENSED FROM "GROWING STRONG AGAIN"

THOSE WHO HOPE IN THE LORD

Will renew their strength.

Will soar on wings like eagles.

Will run and not grow weary.

Will walk and not be faint.

FROM ISAIAH 40:31
"THE HOLY BIBLE"

THE BIBLE

It is *perfect,* restoring the soul.

It is *sure,* making wise the simple.

It is *right,* rejoicing the heart.

It is *pure,* enlightening the eyes.

KING DAVID
ADAPTED FROM PSALM 19:7–8

TIPS FOR MEMORIZING SCRIPTURE

1.
Make it the desire of your heart.

2.
Choose a translation you're comfortable memorizing.

3.
Start with a familiar book, such as Matthew or John.

4.
Be willing to make the sacrifice of time and energy.

5.
Review the memorized portions regularly.

6.
Stay faithful and don't give up.

POLLY HOUSE
FROM "LIFEWISE" MAGAZINE

HOLY HABITS

Look for God's fingerprints in the world and tell others what you see.

Acknowledge His power.

Remember that He is a big God.

Dwell on His love for you.

Ask God to teach you what His gifts to you are each day.

Tell God what you need.

Silence your heart daily so that you can be sensitive to God's presence.

Cleanse your heart daily.

Daily thank God and maintain a constant connection with Him.

Become a communicator of peace to others.

MIMI WILSON AND SHELLY COOK VOLKHARDT
CONDENSED FROM "HOLY HABITS"

ADMINISTRATION
- ∽ I like to organize facts, groups, or events.
- ∽ When working on projects or events, I easily see how to avoid potential problems.
- ∽ I handle details well.

DISCERNMENT
- ∽ I often correctly sense the motives of others.
- ∽ I often get a gut feeling about whether a situation is good or bad.
- ∽ I often sense whether a book/movie/presentation will bring people closer to God—or push them away.

FAITH
- ∽ I know God is faithful, even when life seems impossible.
- ∽ If I sense that God is behind something, I find it easy to support when others have doubts.
- ∽ People often tell me I am an incurable optimist.

ENCOURAGEMENT, COUNSELING, OR MERCY
- ∽ I long to reach out to those who are hurt or rejected.
- ∽ I often see the positive traits in others that they are slow to recognize in themselves.
- ∽ Others say I am a good listener.

SHEPHERDING

- I enjoy encouraging others to develop their faith.
- I would enjoy nurturing and caring for a group of people over time.
- As I consider helping others, I tend to think in terms of groups or teams rather than individuals.

HELPS

- I would rather take on practical tasks than lead.
- I notice what needs to be done and do it, feeling a spiritual link to the ministries I serve.
- I like working behind the scenes.

HOSPITALITY

- I enjoy making people feel welcome.
- I view relationships as opportunities to pass on God's love.
- I can provide safe environments for people in need.

WISDOM

- People often come to me for advice about personal or religious matters.
- Often, I can find a profoundly simple solution in the midst of a difficult situation.
- It is easy for me to make practical application of the truths found in the Bible.

JANE A. G. KISE
FROM "LIFEWISE" MAGAZINE

ALLOWS FOR...

Gratitude in prosperity

Patience in adversity

A wonderful security

JOHN CALVIN
THEOLOGIAN

GOD IS THE ONE WHO...

---

pardons our sins.

refuses to stay angry with us.

delights in showing us mercy.

pours His compassion out on us.

tramples our sins and throws them into the deepest ocean.

shows us His faithfulness.

loves us with an everlasting love.

ADAPTED FROM MICAH 7:18–20
"THE HOLY BIBLE"

FAITH

WORDS OF FAITH

The universe does not make sense without God.
E. STANLEY JONES

❧

If God sends us stony paths,
He will provide us with strong shoes.
ALEXANDER MACLAREN

❧

We must accept finite disappointment,
but we must never lose infinite hope.
MARTIN LUTHER KING JR.

❧

The only way to learn strong faith is to endure strong trials.
GEORGE MÜELLER

❧

Happy and strong and brave shall we be—
able to endure all things, and to do all things—
if we believe that every day, every hour, every moment
of our life is in God's hands.
HENRY VAN DYKE

Faith is the radar that sees through the fog.
CORRIE TEN BOOM

*God needs no one, but when faith is present
He works through anyone.*
A. W. TOZER

Human problems are never greater than divine solutions.
IRWIN LUTZER

God comes in where my helplessness begins.
OSWALD CHAMBERS

God's gifts put man's best dreams to shame.
ELIZABETH BARRETT BROWNING

GOD...

is a giver of life.

is a heart mender.

is a forgiver.

keeps on giving.

grieves.

is a true friend.

is holy.

is the bearer of our burdens.

is our great contentment.

is the redeemer of our pain.

works through our weakness.

brings blessings in the darkness.

is powerful.

restores our innocence.

gives rest.

is worthy of glory.

is our pleasure.

pours out mercy.

satisfies the mind.

meets our needs…and more.

STEVE FRY
ADAPTED FROM "I AM: THE UNVEILING OF GOD"

AARON'S BLESSING

May the LORD bless you

and protect you.

May the LORD smile on you

and be gracious to you.

May the LORD show you his favor

and give you his peace.

NUMBERS 6:24–26
"THE HOLY BIBLE," NLT

Life-Changing Advice in a Quick-to-Read Format!

With sales of over 700,000 copies, the Lists to Live By series has something for everyone—guidance, inspiration, humor, family, love, health, and home. These books are perfect gifts for all occasions.

For the Moments
That Matter Most

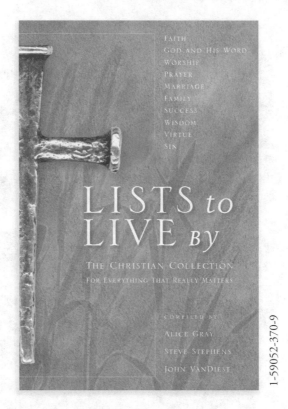

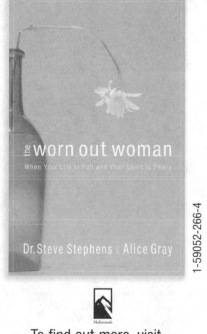

The Stories for the Heart Series

compiled by Alice Gray

ACKNOWLEDGMENTS

Hundreds of books and magazines were researched and dozens of professionals interviewed for this collection. A diligent effort was made to attribute original ownership of each list, and when necessary, obtain permission to reprint. If we have overlooked giving proper credit to anyone, please accept our apologies. If you will contact Multnomah Publishers, Inc., Post Office Box 1720, Sisters, Oregon 97759, with written documentation, corrections will be made prior to additional printings.

Notes and acknowledgments are shown in the order the lists appear in each section of the book. For permission to reprint a list, please request permission from the original source shown in the following bibliography. The editors gratefully acknowledge authors, publishers, and agents who granted permission for reprinting these lists.

SUCCESS

"Seven Principles of Success" by Pat Williams condensed from *Secrets from the Mountain* (Fleming H. Revell, a division of Baker Book House Company), © 2001. Used by permission.

"Barriers to Growth" by Paul J. Meyer from *Unlocking Your Legacy*. Copyright © 2002. Published by Moody Press, a ministry of Moody Bible Institute. Used by permission.

"You and Your Boss" by Steve Marr adapted from *Business Proverbs* (Fleming H. Revell, a division of Baker Book House Company), © 2001. Used by permission.

"Principles of Criticism" by Neil Eskelin condensed from *Leading with Love* (Fleming H. Revell, a division of Baker Book House Company), © 2001. Used by permission.

"What Keeps Us From Dreaming" by Dr. Steve Stephens, psychologist and seminar speaker, Clackamas, Oregon. Used by permission of the author.

"Business Principles" by Steve Marr adapted from *Business Proverbs* (Fleming H. Revell, a division of Baker Book House Company), © 2001. Used by permission.

"Tools That Organized People Use" taken from: *Finding More Time in Your Life*. Copyright © 2001 by Dru Scott Decker. Published by Harvest House Publishers, Eugene, OR 97402. Used by permission.

"Reminders for Leaders" by Neil Eskelin condensed from *Leading with Love* (Fleming H. Revell, a division of Baker Book House Company), © 2001. Used by permission.

"Qualities of a Great Mentor" by Gary Collins from *Christian Coaching* (NavPress). Copyright © 2001. Used by permission.

"What a Mentor Can Help You Do" by Gary Collins condensed from *Christian*

Coaching (NavPress). Copyright © 2001. Used by permission.

"Personal Goal Setting" by Craig Jutila condensed from *Leadership Essentials for Chldren's Ministry* (Group Publishing, Inc.). Copyright © 2002. Used by permission.

"How to Find Your Passion" by Gary Collins condensed from *Christian Coaching* (NavPress). Copyright © 2001. Used by permission.

"Influential People" by Dr. Steve Stephens, psychologist and seminar speaker, Clackamas, Oregon. Used by permission of the author.

"The Successful Person" by Glenda Hotton, M.A., C.D.C., M.F.T., counselor specializing in women's issues of trauma, physical abuse, and relationships/substance abuse in private practice in Newhall, California. Used by permission of the author.

"Seven Myths about Success" taken from: *Finding More Time in Your Life*. Copyright © 2001 by Dru Scott Decker. Published by Harvest House Publishers, Eugene, OR 97402. Used by permission.

"How to Remember What You Read" by Kyle Liedtke, copyright © 2002. Used by permission of the author. Kyle Liedtke is president of Mediatalk (media training, media production, media relations), mediatalkcom@aol.com.

"Seven Ways to Gain Influence" by Dale Galloway, condensed from: *On-Purpose Leadership*. Copyright © 2001, Beacon Hill Press of Kansas City, MO. Used by permission.

DAY BY DAY

"Things to Do Every Day" by Dr. Steve Stephens, psychologist and seminar speaker, Clackamas, Oregon. Used by permission of the author.

"Tips for Life" from "Dear Ann Landers." Permission granted by Ann Landers and Creators Syndicate.

"Watch Your Attitude" from *Highlighted in Yellow* by H. Jackson Brown Jr. and Rochelle Pennington, and published by Rutledge Hill Press, Nashville, Tennessee.

"40 Often Overlooked Blessings" from *The Simple Abudance Journal of Gratitude* by Sarah Ban Breathnach. Copyright © 1996 by Sarah Ban Breathnach. By permission of Warner Books, Inc.

"Simplicity…" by Dr. Steve Stephens, psychologist and seminar speaker, Clackamas, Oregon. Used by permission of the author.

"Side Effects of Worrying" by Paul J. Meyer from *Unlocking Your Legacy*. Copyright © 2002. Published by Moody Press, a ministry of Moody Bible Institute. Used by permission.

"When It's Hard to Get Up" from *Threefold Technique for a Great Morning* by Dr. Ray Stedman. Used by permission of Elaine Stedman.

"Ten Habits to Memorize and Live By" from *Get Your Act Together* by Pam Young. Copyright © 1993 by Pamela I. Young and Peggy A. Jones. Reprinted by permission of HarperCollins Publishers, Inc.

"Enrich Your Life" from *Inner Peace for Busy People* by Joan Borysenko, Ph.D. Copyright © 2001. Published by Hay House, Inc., Carlsbad, CA.

"Ten Life-Defining Moments" by James Emery White. Reprinted from *Life-Defining Moments*. Copyright © 2001 by James Emery White. Used by permission of WaterBrook Press, Colorado Springs, CO. All rights reserved.

"Take Time for Silence" by Pastor Curtis Tucker, Redmond, OR. Used by permission of the author.

"The Simplest Pleasures of Life" by LaVerna Klippenstein, adapted from an article in *Christian Living* magazine. Used by permission of the author.

"Ten Uncommon Delights" by Dr. Steve Stephens, psychologist and seminar speaker, Clackamas, Oregon. Used by permission of the author.

RELATIONSHIPS

"Love Is…" by Danae Jacobson from *Things I've Learned Lately*. Published by Multnomah Publishers, Inc., Sisters, OR, © 2001. Used by permission.

"Ten Ways to Celebrate Friendship" by Catherine Stier. Adapted from "Ways to Celebrate Friendship" appearing in the February 10, 2002 issue of *Woman's Day* magazine. Used by permission. All rights reserved.

"Trust Busters" by Dr. Carol Clifton, Ph.D., psychologist, Clackamas, Oregon. Used by permission of the author.

"Trust Builders" by Dr. Carol Clifton, Ph.D., psychologist, Clackamas, Oregon. Used by permission of the author.

"Showing Love" by Tami Stephens, Clackamas, OR. Used by permission of the author.

"When You're Feeling Lonely" by Rhonda Rhea, condensed from *Today's Christian Woman* magazine. Used by permission of the author. Rhonda Rhea is a columnist and feature writer for Christian publications in the U.S. and Canada. She's also a popular conference speaker, and her new book, *Amusing Grace* (Cook Communications), will be out in March 2003.

"Friendship Checkup" by Pam Farrel from *Woman of Confidence*. Copyright © 2001. Published by InterVarsity Press, Downers Grove, IL. Used by permission of the publisher.

"How to Handle Criticism" by Kyle Liedtke, copyright © 2002. Used by permission of the author. Kyle Liedtke is president of Mediatalk (media training, media production, media relations), mediatalkcom@aol.com.

"The Four-Way Test" by Herbert J. Taylor, Rotary International President, 1954–1955. Used by permission.

"Seven Steps That Lead to Problems" by Jack and Carole Mayhall condensed from *Discipleship Journal* magazine. Used by permission of the authors.

"When Someone Hurts Your Feelings" by Pastor Mark Belokonny, Vancouver, WA. Used by permission of the author.

"How to Show Respect" by Tami Stephens, Clackamas, OR. Used by permission of the author.

"What Good Friends Do" by Alice Gray, Dr. Steve Stephens, and John Van Diest. Used by permission of the authors.

"Without Love…" by Pastor Mark Belokonny, Vancouver, WA. Used by permission of the author.

"Keys to Kindness" condensed from *Highlighted in Yellow* by H. Jackson Brown Jr. and Rochelle Pennington, and published by Rutledge Hill Press, Nashville, Tennessee.

"Together" by Dr. Steve Stephens, psychologist and seminar speaker, Clackamas, Oregon. Used by permission of the author.

MARRIAGE

"Rules for Marriage" condensed from *The Rules for Marriage* by Ellen Fein. Copyright © 2001 by Ellen Fein and Sherrie Schneider. By permission of Warner Books, Inc.

"Is Your Marriage a Covenant or a Contract?" from *Covenant Marriage* by Fred Lowery. Copyright © 2002. Used by permission of Howard Publishing Co., West Monroe, LA.

"Ten Ways to Show Your Husband Respect" adapted from *Different by Design* by H. Dale Burke, as printed in *Marriage Partnership* magazine. Used by permission of Moody Press.

"Ten Ways to Show Your Wife Honor" adapted from *Different by Design* by H. Dale Burke, as printed in *Marriage Partnership* magazine. Used by permission of Moody Press.

"Seven Loves of Marriage" by Thomas and Nanette Kinkade condensed from *The Many Loves of Marriage*. Published by Multnomah Publishers, Inc., Sisters, OR, © 2001. Used by permission.

"Romantic Tips for Travelers" by George and Valerie Stuart. Used by permission of the authors.

"Seven Ways to Flirt With Your Spouse" taken from *100 Fun and Fabulous Ways to Flirt with Your Spouse*. Copyright © 2000 by Doug Fields. Published by Harvest House Publishers, Eugene, OR, 97402. Used by permission.

"Every Husband Should Ask His Wife…" by Bob Reccord from *Beneath the Surface*. Copyright © 2002. Used by permission of Broadman & Holman Publishers, Nashville, TN.

"Every Wife Should Ask Her Husband…" by Bob Reccord from *Beneath the Surface*. Copyright © 2002. Used by permission of Broadman & Holman Publishers, Nashville, TN.

"Create Quality Time" by Kay Coles James adapted from *What I Wish I'd Known Before I Got Married*. Published by Multnomah Publishers, Inc., Sisters, OR, © 2001. Used by permission.

"Time Together" by Tim Gardner. This article first appeared in *Marriage Partnership* magazine (spring 2002), published by Christianity Today, Int'l., Carol Stream, Illinois. Dr. Tim Alan Gardner is the director of the Marriage Education and Policy Center at the Indiana Family Institute. He is the author of the book *Sacred Sex: A Spiritual Celebration of Oneness in Marriage*.

"Don'ts of Marriage" by Glenda Hotton, M.A., C.D.C., M.F.T., counselor specializing in women's issues of trauma, physical abuse, and relationships/substance abuse in private practice in Newhall, California. Used by permission of the author.

"Do's of Marriage" by Glenda Hotton, M.A., C.D.C., M.F.T., counselor special-izing in women's issues of trauma, physical abuse, and relationships/substance abuse in private practice in Newhall, California. Used by permission of the author.

"How to Listen" from *Covenant Marriage* by Fred Lowery. Copyright © 2002. Used by permission of Howard Publishing Co., West Monroe, LA.

"When Times Are Tough" by Kay Coles James from *What I Wish I'd Known Before I Got Married.* Published by Multnomah Publishers, Inc., Sisters, OR, © 2001. Used by permission.

"Inappropriate Behaviors" from *Covenant Marriage* by Fred Lowery. Copyright © 2002. Used by permission of Howard Publishing Co., West Monroe, LA.

"How Do You Rate?" by Bob Reccord from *Beneath the Surface.* Copyright © 2002. Used by permission of Broadman & Holman Publishers, Nashville, TN.

"What Makes Marriage Worthwhile?" by David & Claudia Arp condensed from *The Second Half of Marriage.* Used by permission of the authors. David & Claudia Arp, founders of Marriage Alive, are speakers, columnists, and authors of numerous books including *The Second Half of Marriage* and *10 Great Dates.* Web site: www.mar-riagealive.com.

VIRTUE

"Pride vs. Humility" by Pastor Mark Belokonny, Vancouver, WA. Used by per-mission of the author.

"Six Steps to Break a Bad Habit" by Dr. Joseph C. Aldrich, Portland, OR. Used by permission of the author.

"Take Courage" adapted from *Renewing the Soul of America* by Charles Crismier. Copyright © 2002. Published by Elijah Books, Richmond, VA. Used by permission of the author.

"Integrity Is..." by Marty Williams, Portland, OR. Used by permission of the author.

"How to Achieve True Humility" adapted from *The Solomon Secrets.* Copyright © 2002 by Robert Jeffress. Used by permission of WaterBrook Press, Colorado Springs, CO. All rights reserved.

"Developing Self-Discipline" by Dr. John MacArthur. Used by permission of the author and Wolgemuth & Associates, Inc.

"The Test of a Good Principle" adapted from *Renewing the Soul of America* by Charles Crismier. Copyright © 2002. Published by Elijah Books, Richmond, VA. Used by permission of the author.

"Protecting Your Values" by Bob Reccord condensed from *Beneath the Surface.* Copyright © 2002. Used by permission of Broadman & Holman Publishers, Nashville, TN.

"Cultivate These Qualities" from *The Challenge of the Disciplined Life* by Richard J. Foster. Copyright © 1985 by Richard J. Foster. Reprinted by permission of Harper Collins Publishers, Inc. and William Neill-Hall Ltd.

"Eight Valuable Disciplines" by Gary L. Thomas adapted from *Authentic Faith*. Copyright © 2002. Used by permission of the author.

HEALTH

"Regular Exercise" by U.S. Department of Health and Human Services.

"Taking Your Medicine" by John Cooper, Redmond, OR. Used by permission of the author.

"Before You Take Any Kind of Medicine…" by U.S. Food and Drug Administration.

"Ten Signs of Burnout" by Dr. Steve Stephens, psychologist and seminar speaker, Clackamas, Oregon. Used by permission of the author.

"How to Find Relief From Burnout" by Rhonda Rhea. Used by permission of the author. Rhonda Rhea is a columnist and feature writer for Christian publications in the U.S. and Canada. She's also a popular conference speaker, and her new book, *Amusing Grace* (Cook Communications), will be out in March 2003.

"Ten Ways to Relieve the Pressure" reprinted by permission, *Rev* magazine. Copyright © 2001, Group Publishing, Inc., Box 481, Loveland, CO 80539.

"How to Avoid Getting Sick" by U.S. Food and Drug Administration.

"Advantages of Walking" condensed from *Stressbusters* by Kathrine Butler. Copyright © 1998 by Kathrine Butler. This material is used by permission of John Wiley & Sons, Inc.

"Nine Ways to Spice Up Your Workout" by Elizabeth Pope from *New Choices* magazine. Copyright © 2002 by RD Publications, Inc. Used by permission of the author.

"Living the Good Life" condensed from *Living the Good Life* by Ruth McGinnis. Published by Fleming H. Revell, a division of Baker Book House. Copyright © 2001. Used by permission of the publisher.

"Eating Well" condensed from *Living the Good Life* by Ruth McGinnis. Published by Fleming H. Revell, a division of Baker Book House. Copyright © 2001. Used by permission of the publisher.

"Help Your Children Build Strong Bones By:" by Genetta Adair from *Focus on the Family* magazine. Used by permission of the author. Genetta Adair is a freelance writer and lives in Tennessee with her husband, two children, and yellow Labrador Retriever.

"Stress Breaks at Work" from *You Don't Have to Go Home from Work Exhausted* by Ann McGee-Cooper. Copyright © 1992. Published by Bantam Books, a division of Random House, Inc., New York, NY. Used by permission of the publisher.

"The Balancing Act" by Ragan Communications, Inc., Chicago, IL. Used by permission of the publisher.

"How to Chill Out" reprinted by permission, *Rev* magazine. Copyright © 2001, Group Publishing, Inc., Box 481, Loveland, CO 80539.

"Letting Go of Worries" by Pam Vredevelt adapted from *Letting Go of Worry and Anxiety*. Published by Multnomah Publishers, Inc., Sisters, OR, © 2001. Used by permission.

"Anxiety Cure" from *The Anxiety Cure: You Can Find Emotional Tranquility and Wholeness* by Archibald Hart. Copyright © 1999 by Archibald D. Hart, W Publishing Group, Nashville, Tennessee. All rights reserved.

THE SECOND HALF

"Five Tips for Staying Young" from *The Tale of the Tardy Oxcart* by Charles R. Swindoll. Copyright © 1998 by Charles R. Swindoll, W Publishing Group, Nashville, Tennessee. All rights reserved.

"Romance after the Kids Leave Home" by David and Claudia Arp from *LifeWise* magazine. Used by permission of the authors. David and Claudia Arp founded Marriage Alive, are speakers, columnists, and authors of numerous books including *The Second Half of Marriage* and *10 Great Dates*. Web site: www.marriagealive.com.

"Adjusting to Your Spouse's Retirement" by Mary Ann Cook adapted from *LifeWise* magazine as printed in *Better Life!* Used by permission of the author. Mary Ann Cook conducts seminars for women with retired or work-at-home husbands. Her book is due out soon from Focus on the Family. Contact her at www.maryanncook.com or P.O. Box 300008, Escondido, CA 92030.

"Enjoy Your Retirement" by Rich Schmidt, Ph.D., Redmond, OR. Used by permission of the author.

"Revitalize Your Retirement Routines" by Charlotte Adelsperger, Overland Park, KS. Copyright © 2002. Used by permission of the author.

"20 Reasons Grandparents Are Important" compiled by the editors. Used by permission.

"Ten Ways to Touch Grandkids from Afar" by Barbara Baumgardner condensed from *The Tie That Binds* as published in *RV Companion* magazine. Used by permission of the author. Barbara Baumgardner, with golden retriever companion, Molly, treks around the country in a motor home in search of interesting people and places to write about in her *RV Companion* column.

"Do's and Don'ts of Grandparenting" by Becky Stephens, Clackamas, OR. Used by permission of the author.

"How Grandparents Can Encourage Grandchildren" from *The Essential Grandparent* by Dr. Lillian Carson. Copyright © 1996 by Dr. Lillian Carson. Published by Health Communications, Inc., Deerfield Beach, FL. Used by permission of the publisher.

"Successful Volunteering" from *Catch the Spirit!* by The Prudential Spirit of Community Initiative. Used by permission.

"Keep Life Upbeat" by Paul J. Meyer from *Unlocking Your Legacy*. Copyright © 2002. Published by Moody Press, a ministry of Moody Bible Institute. Used by permission.

"Cultivate an Active Mind" condensed from *Go the Distance* by Ed Rowell. Copyright © 2002. Published by Broadman and Holman Publishers, Nashville, TN. Used by permission of the publisher.

"Things I Wish I'd Done Sooner" by Barbara M. Darland, retired English professor at Multnomah Bible College in Portland, Oregon. Currently Barbara is a proofreader, speaker, and artist. Used by permission. Copyright © 2002.

"Leaving a Legacy" by Paul J. Meyer condensed from *Unlocking Your Legacy*. Copyright © 2002. Published by Moody Press, a ministry of Moody Bible Institute. Used by permission.

"Things Spouses Need to Do While Both Are Healthy" by Rich Schmidt, Ph.D., Redmond, OR. Used by permission of the author.

"Aging" by Tress Van Diest, Portland, OR. Used by permission of the author.

TOUGH TIMES

"God's Mercy" © Cook Communications Ministries, *Dare to Trust, Dare to Hope Again* by Kari West. Reprinted with permission. May not be further reproduced. All rights reserved.

"What Survivors Say" taken from: *Will My Life Ever Be the Same?* Copyright © 2002 by H. Norman Wright. Published by Harvest House Publishers, Eugene, OR 97402. Used by permission.

"Emotional Healing Takes Time" adapted from *Starting Over* by Thomas A. Whiteman, Ph.D., and Randy Petersen. Copyright © 2001. Published by Piñon Press, Colorado Springs, CO. Used by permission of the publisher.

"Staying Married through Tragedies" by Don Harting, Liverpool, NY. First published in *Marriage Partnership* magazine, summer 2001. Used by permission of the author.

"Getting Back on Track" condensed from *Go the Distance* by Ed Rowell. Copyright © 2002. Published by Broadman and Holman Publishers, Nashville, TN. Used by permission of the publisher.

"When Our Children Disappoint Us" by Barbara Baumgardner condensed from *Decision* magazine. Used by permission of the author. Barbara Baumgardner is the author of *A Passage through Grief*, of which 10,000 copies were sent to the survivors of the World Trade Center tragedy. She also wrote *A Passage through Divorce*. Her e-mail is mollyb@bendcable.com.

"If Your Friend Is Chronically Ill" by Stacey S. Padrick adapted from *Discipleship Journal* magazine. Used by permission of the author. Stacey is the author of *Living with Mystery: Finding God in the Midst of Unanswered Questions* (Bethany House Publishers, © 2001).

"How to Be Unsinkable" condensed from *Unsinkable* by Pat Williams. Published by Fleming H. Revell, a division of Baker Book House. Copyright © 2002. Used by permission of the publisher.

"Steps to Help a Grieving Child" taken from: *Will My Life Ever Be the Same?* Copyright © 2002 by H. Norman Wright. Published by Harvest House Publishers, Eugene, OR 97402. Used by permission.

"Seven Holiday Gifts for the Grieving" by Barbara Baumgardner. Copyright © 1994. Used by permission of the author. Barbara Baumgardner is the author of *A Passage through Grief*, of which 10,000 copies were sent to the survivors of the World Trade Center tragedy. She also wrote *A Passage Through Divorce*. Her e-mail is mollyb@bendcable.com.

"An Attitude toward Pain" from *Starting Over* by Thomas A. Whiteman, Ph.D. and Randy Petersen. Copyright © 2001. Published by Piñon Press, Colorado Springs, CO. Used by permission of the publisher.

FAMILY LIFE

"You're Missing the Truly Important Stuff If…" by David J. Stipech from *Focus on the Family* magazine. Used by permission of the author. Bringing encouragement to people is at the heart of David J. Stipech's speaking and writing. For information on David's published resources and speaking on effective work, life, and family, e-mail him at david@thepeoplecenter.net.

"Things to Remember as a New Mom" by Tania Gray, Lake Havasu City, AZ. Used by permission of the author.

"What I Wish I'd Known" by Kay Coles James condensed from *What I Wish I'd Known Before I Got Married.* Published by Multnomah Publishers, Inc., Sisters, OR, © 2001. Used by permission.

"Three T's For Your Family" by Dennis and Barbara Rainey condensed from *Growing a Spiritually Strong Family.* Published by Multnomah Publishers, Inc., Sisters, OR, © 2002. Used by permission.

"What Good Families Are Doing Right" condensed from *The Family.* Copyright © 2002 by Dorthy Kelley Patterson. Published by Broadman & Holman Publishers, Nashville, Tennessee. Used by permission of the publisher. All rights reserved

"25 Ways to Say 'I Love You' to Your Child" by Renee Bacher condensed from *Parents* magazine.

"Making Family Meals Successful" by Mimi Knight condensed from *Christian Parenting Today* magazine. This article first appeared in *Christian Parenting Today* magazine (Jan./Feb. 2002) published by Christianity Today Int'l, Carol Stream, IL. Used by permission of the author.

"Making Family Meals Fun" by Mimi Knight condensed from *Christian Parenting Today* magazine. This article first appeared in *Christian Parenting Today* magazine (Jan./Feb. 2002) published by Christianity Today Int'l, Carol Stream, IL. Used by permission of the author.

"Self-Esteem Builders" by Betsy Cañas Garmon from *ParentLife* magazine. Used by permission of the author. Betsy Cañas Garmon is a mother, artist, and homemaker. She and Randy have five children.

"Resisting Temptation" by Carla Williams condensed from *Focus on the Family* magazine. Used by permission of the author.

"Managing Conflict" by Victor Parachin condensed from *ParentLife* magazine. Copyright © 1999. Used by permission of the publisher.

"Squelching Sibling Squabbles" by Debbie D. Gregory condensed from *ParentLife* magazine. Used by permission of the author.

"How to Spot a Troubled Child" by Wesley Sharpe, Ed.D., from *HomeLife* magazine, February 2000. Used by permission of the author.

"Successful Parents…" adapted from *The Solomon Secrets.* Copyright © 2002 by

Robert Jeffress. Used by permission of WaterBrook Press, Colorado Springs, CO. All right reserved.

"12 Helps for Long-Distance Travel with Children" by Barbara Baumgardner. Used by permission of the author. Barbara Baumgardner, with golden retriever companion, Molly, treks around the country in a motor home in search of interesting people and places to write about in her *RV Companion* column.

"A Great Parent…" compiled by Ron Taffel, Ph.D., from *Parents* magazine.

"Small Gestures of Big Love" by Carly Carter from *ParentLife* magazine. Used by permission of the author. Carly Carter lives in Michigan and is an author of children's books.

FAMILY LESSONS

"How to Handle a Bully" by Dylan Stephens, Clackamas, OR. Used by permission of the author.

"15 Questions Parents Should Ask Their Teens" adapted from *Mom! I Feel Fat!* Copyright © 2001 by Sharon A. Hersh. Used by permission of WaterBrook Press, Colorado Springs, CO. All rights reserved.

"Qualities to Build in Your Children" from *Neat Mom, Messie Kids* by Sandra Felton. Published by Fleming H. Revell, a division of Baker Book House. Copyright © 2002. Used by permission of the publisher.

"Eight Fun Ways to Teach Values" by Pamela Kramer condensed from *Parents* magazine © October 2001, Gruner & Jahr USA Publishing. Reprinted from *Parents* magazine by permission.

"30 Rules of Neatness" condensed from *Neat Mom, Messie Kids* by Sandra Felton. Published by Fleming H. Revell, a division of Baker Book House. Copyright © 2002. Used by permission of the publisher.

"Maxims of Maturity" adapted from *Help for the Harried Homeschooler.* Copyright © 2002 by Christine M. Field. Used by permission of WaterBrook Press, Colorado Springs, CO. All rights reserved.

"When Your Child Wants to Give Up" taken from *The Parent Survival Guide* by Dr. Todd Cartmell. Copyright © 2001 by Dr. Todd Cartmell. Used by permission of Zondervan.

"How to Juggle Family Demands" by Rhonda Rhea condensed from the *St. Louis Family Gazette.* Used by permission of the author. Rhonda Rhea is a columnist and feature writer for Christian publications in the U.S. and Canada. She's also a popular conference speaker and her new book, *Amusing Grace* (Cook Communications), will be out in March 2003.

"When Your Child Oversteps Boundaries" by June Hunt, Dallas, TX. Used by permission of the author.

"The Power of Consequences" by Suzanne Woods Fisher, contributing editor to *Christian Parenting Today.* This article first appeared in *Christian Parenting Today* (Jan./Feb. 2002). Used by permission of the author.

"Building Can-Do Kids" condensed from *Raising Resilient Children* by Dr. Robert

Brooks and Dr. Sam Goldstein. Used with permission of The McGraw-Hill Companies, Inc.

"Appreciating Your Kids' Teachers" by Alice Gray, compiler of *Stories for a Teacher's Heart*. Used by permission of the author.

"How Your Kids Can Make a Positive Impression with Teachers" by Tania Gray, Lake Havesu City, AZ. Used by permission of the author.

"Teaching Kids about Money" by Lisa Jackson adapted from *Christian Parenting Today* magazine. Used by permission of the author. This article first appeared in *Christian Parenting Today* magazine (March/April 2002), published by Christianity Today, Int'l., Carol Stream, Illinois.

"Seven Strategies to Build a Strong Work Ethic" by Barbara Curtis condensed from *Christian Parenting Today* magazine. Used by permission of the author. Barbara Curtis, an award-winning author with two published books and over 500 articles, finds tons of material as mother to 12 children, grandmother to 8 (so far!). Visit her at www.barbaracurtis.com. This article first appeared in *Christian Parenting Today* magazine (January/February 2002), published by Christianity Today, Int'l., Carol Stream, Illinois.

"Seven Ideas for Young Entrepreneurs" by Robin Popp from *HomeLife* magazine. Used by permission of the author.

"Helpful Friend-Finding Tips" by Susie Larson condensed from *Focus on the Family* magazine. Used by permission of the author. Susie Larson is an author, speaker, and freelance writer for Focus on the Family.

WISDOM

"Ten Things That Really Matter" by Dr. Joseph C. Aldrich, Portland, OR. Used by permission of the author.

"Where Can I Find Good Advice?" by Robert S. Bobosky, businessman, Portland, Oregon. Used by permission of the author.

"Principles to Live By" by author unknown. Excerpted from *Dare to Trust, Dare to Hope Again* by Kari West, © 2001 by Cook Communications Ministries. Reprinted with permission. May not be further reproduced. All rights reserved.

"Ten Ways to Speak the Truth" by Dr. Steve Stephens, psychologist and seminar speaker, Clackamas, Oregon. Used by permission of the author.

"The More You Have" by Randy Alcorn condensed from *The Treasure Principle*. Published by Multnomah Publishers, Inc., Sisters, OR, © 2001. Used by permission.

"Don't Let Money Control You" condensed from *My Own Worst Enemy* by Alan Nelson. Published by Fleming H. Revell, a division of Baker Book House. Copyright © 2001. Used by permission of the publisher.

"Tips for Smart Living" by Debra-Lee S. Levesque, Lebanon, ME. Used by permission of the author.

"Things I've Learned Lately" by Danae Jacobson adapted from *Things I've Learned Lately*. Published by Multnomah Publishers, Inc., Sisters, OR, © 2001. Used by permission.

"When Making Your Decisions" adapted from *Renewing the Soul of America* by Charles Crismier. Copyright © 2002. Published by Elijah Books, Richmond, VA. Used by permission of the author.

"12 Powerful Words" by John Van Diest, associate publisher. Used by permission of the author.

"Beware Of…" by Dr. Steve Stephens, psychologist and seminar speaker, Clackamas, Oregon. Used by permission of the author.

"What You Deserve" by H. Dale Burke, Fullerton, CA. Used by permission of the author.

FAITH

"What God Gives" by Dr. Steve Stephens, psychologist and seminar speaker, Clackamas, Oregon. Used by permission of the author.

"Five Kinds of God Moments" by Alan D. Wright from *The God Moment Principle*. Published by Multnomah Publishers, Inc., Sisters, OR, © 1999. Used by permission.

"Understanding Hope" by Charles B. Darland, retired college professor of aviation at Mt. Hood Community College, currently building his own airplane. Used by permission. © 2002.

"When You Trust God" from *Strengthening Your Grip* by Charles Swindoll. Copyright © 1998 by Charles Swindoll. W Publishing Group, Nashville, Tennessee. All rights reserved.

"What Faith Is" by Pamela Reeve from *Faith Is…* Published by Multnomah Publishers, Inc., Sisters, OR, © 1999. Used by permission.

"What Faith Does" condensed from *Growing Strong Again* by Gregory Jantz. Published by Fleming H. Revell, a division of Baker Book House. Copyright © 1998. Used by permission of the publisher.

"Tips for Memorizing Scripture" by Polly House from *LifeWise* magazine, copyright © 2000. Used by permission of the publisher.

"Holy Habits" condensed from *Holy Habits* by Mimi Wilson and Shelly Cook Volkhardt. Copyright © 1999. Used by permission of NavPress, Colorado Springs, CO.

"Assessing Your Spiritual Gifts" by Jane A. G. Kise from *LifeWise* magazine. Used by permission of the author. Jane Kise is a freelance writer from Minnesota. Her books include *Life Keys: Who You Are, Why You're Here, What You Do Best,* and *Did You Get What You Prayed For?*

"The Unveiling of God" by Steve Fry adapted from *I Am: The Unveiling of God.* Published by Multnomah Publishers, Inc., Sisters, OR, © 2000. Used by permission.